Shocking Entertainment

Viewer Response to Violent Movies

To Don Butler

Shocking Entertainment

Viewer Response to Violent Movies

Annette Hill

UNIVERSITY UP of JL LUTON PRESS

British Library Cataloguing in Publication Data
A catalogue record for this book is available from the British Library

ISBN: 1 86020 525 9

Published by
John Libbey Media
Faculty of Humanities
University of Luton
75 Castle Street
Luton
Bedfordshire LU1 3AJ
United Kingdom
Tel: +44 (0) 1582 743297; Fax: +44 (0) 1582 743298
e-mail: john.libbey@luton.ac.uk

Cover Design by Visual Imagination Ltd
Typeset in Adobe Garamond
Printed in Great Britain by Gwynprint Ltd, Haywards Heath, West Sussex

Contents

List of Tables and Figures   vi

Acknowledgements   vii

1   Introduction: Researching response to viewing violence   1

2   Designing the study   7

3   Consumer choice and violent movies   19
   Hype, Scandal and Cultural Cachet
   Hollywood Versus New Brutalism

4   The activity of viewing violence   27
   Audience Awareness
   Physical and Emotional Responses
   The Role of Anticipation

5   Building character relationships   39
   The Question of Identification
   Context and Characterization
   Personal Experience and Imagination

6   Thresholds and self-censorship   51
   Social and Personal Thresholds
   Self-censoring Violence
   Boundary Testing

7   The question of entertainment   75
   Response to Real Violence
   The Safety of Cinema

8   Reservoir Dogs: A case study   85
           Societal/Cultural Factors
           Mr Blonde and Marvin
           Audio/Visual Effects
           Effects of Repeated Viewing

9   Summary and conclusion   99

           Appendices   111
           1: Guiding questions for focus groups
           2: List of target films used in focus groups
           3: Registration form – focus groups

           References   117

           Index   123

Tables and Figures

Table 1:   Target Films   10
Table 2a–c: CAA Film Profile – Gender, Class, Age   14
Table 3:   Viewing Figures for Target Films   19
Table 4:   UK Box Office Grosses, 1996   20
Table 5:   Reading Figures for Popular Newspapers/Magazines   20
Table 6:   Repeated Viewing Figures   25
Table 7:   Cinema Viewing Figures   63
Table 8:   Video Viewing Figures   63
Table 9:   Video Retail Unit Figures   63

Figure 1:   *Henry, Portrait of a Serial Killer:* 'Becky and Henry'   42
Figure 2:   *True Romance* 'Alabama'   54
Figure 3:   *Man Bites Dog:* 'Ben, the serial killer'   84
Figure 3:   *Reservoir Dogs:* 'Mr Blonde'   91
Figure 4:   *Reservoir Dogs:* 'Marvin, Mr White and Mr Pink'   94

Acknowledgements

The research in this study was funded by Roehampton Institute London. I would like to thank Professor Ann Thompson and Professor Bryan Loughrey for their help and support. I would also like to thank the English Department Office for expertly fielding queries and helping with administration.

A special thanks must go to Kevin Bales for suggesting I try focus groups in the first place, and then patiently telling me how to do it. I would also like to thank John Thompson for invaluable help with the writing of this study and for agreeing to read the final draft, and to Kevin McCarron for constructive comments with regard to the manuscript. Thanks must go to Alison Fellows and Ian Calcutt for checking the quirks and foibles in the final manuscript. Thanks also to Manuel Alvarado and David Gauntlett for trusting me to do a good job.

Special thanks and love to Don Butler for acting as assistant moderator even though it was his day off, and for always being there. And a final thank you must go to all the people who agreed to come to the Green Door and talk about their experiences: they are the real stars of the show.

Thanks to Electric Pictures for permission to use quotations and video sales figures, and to reproduce film stills from *Henry, Portrait of a Serial Killer*. Thanks to Polygram for permission to use quotations from *Reservoir Dogs*, and to use video sales figures for *Reservoir Dogs* and *Killing Zoe*. Thanks to Pictorial Press for permission to reproduce films stills from *Reservoir Dogs*. Thanks to Bueno Vista Home Entertainment for permission to use video sales figures for *Pulp Fiction*. Thanks to Polygram Video, on behalf of Guild Film Distribution, for permission to use video sales figures for *Bad Lieutenant*. Thanks also to *Screen International* for supplying UK box office figures at short notice and to the Cinema Advertising Association for a demographic breakdown of moviegoers and the target films.

1

Introduction: Researching response to viewing violence

Dustin Hoffman has had enough. The star of *Straw Dogs* (Sam Peckinpah, 1971), perhaps one of the most notorious violent movies of the 1970s, believes our contemporary society is saturated with screen violence. He says: 'I look at a script and if it has what I think is gratuitous violence I won't do it' (Hoffman, 1996, p.6). Whilst on holiday in Guatemala, I went to see *Straw Dogs* in a video bar. There were four of us. Outside, the presence of military hardware was an unsettling sight, with guns watching you from the supermarket checkout. But it didn't stop us enjoying the film. After all, it was only a movie.

Here is an example of two very different viewpoints. On the one hand, there is Dustin Hoffman who believes watching screen violence can cause violent behaviour, and on the other hand there is me, a moviegoer who enjoys watching violent movies. We appear to be polar opposites. If our opinions of screen violence were to be discussed by the press, an article would look something like this: Hoffman would be on the right hand side of the page, myself, on the left, and the article would do its best to make our discussion appear antagonistic and divided. 'Does watching screen violence make you violent?', the article asks – Hoffman says yes, I say no. Of course, there is no evidence to suggest either is right, this is merely an exhibition of personal opinions.

What I want to suggest in this book is that there are more productive ways to debate screen violence. By productive, I mean that there are areas of investigation other than the cause-effect debate, which will prove useful to those interested in the process of viewing violence.[1] The question I want to ask is: why do people wish to see violent movies? It is only once we discover why watching violent movies is a popular leisure activity that we can begin to understand the complex emotional responses to viewing violence. Consequently, rather than focusing on the movies themselves, and debating what the body count is in *Natural Born Killers* (Oliver Stone, 1995), it seems logical to talk to consumers of violent movies and see what they have to say

---

1. For research into behavioural effects see, Barlow and Hill (1985), Newson (1994), Wiegman, Kuttschreuter, and Baarda (1992) amongst others. For discussion of the 'effects' debate see, Tulloch and Tulloch (1992), Cumberbatch and Howitt (1989), Buckingham and Allerton (1996b), Barker (1984) amongst others. For an overview of audience research see, Docherty, Morrison and Tracey (1987), Livingstone (1990), Seiter, Borchers, Kreutzner, and Warth (1989), Moores (1993), Mayne (1993) for film theory, and Palmer (1986) for children's responses.

about screen violence. Therefore, my research is concerned with emotional responses to violent movies, not behavioural effects, and it aims to encourage a more open forum for debate with regard to the issue of violence, a debate which can incorporate a variety of responses and is not restricted to an either/or scenario.[2]

I am not the first to suggest that the cause-effect model is non-productive. David Gauntlett (1995) makes no bones about contesting the dubious state of the 'effects' debate. Gauntlett's book, *Moving Experiences*, provides an overview of behaviourial effects research and concludes that such research is neither reliable nor valid.[3] He argues that the 'effects tradition has reached the end of [a] circuitous, and theoretically undernourished line of enquiry'(p.7). Indeed, if it were not for media interest in the cause-effect model, most recently fuelled by Elizabeth Newson (1994) and her 'report' on screen violence, contemporary researchers could devote their time to more constructive methods of enquiry.[4] As it is, the 'effects' debate demands attention because the media give it attention.

And, of course, I am not the first to focus on the viewer as a source of constructive information with regard to understanding film and television. Media studies has long since acknowledged that the TV viewer is not a passive couch potato, but an active observer (See Singer and Singer [1983], Gauntlett [1995], Buckingham [1993a, 1993b, 1996a], Moores [1993], Kidd-Hewitt et al [1995]), although to judge by the representation of viewers of violent movies in the media, this popular misconception is still prevalent. One only has to look at coverage of the V-chip debate in Britain in March 1996 to realise the extent of the 'passive viewer' mythology.[5] The V-chip is designed so that parents can regulate the viewing habits of their children; this assumes that children cannot regulate their own viewing habits, whereas a growing body of evidence (see Buckingham [1996a], Barratt [1996], Gauntlett [1997]) indi-

---

2.   There has been a great deal of research into emotional responses to television in recent years. Perhaps one of the best know researchers in this area is David Buckingham who has published a number of extremely interesting studies into children's emotional responses to television – see, Buckingham (1993a, 1993b, 1996a). However, other researchers are also investigating different emotional responses and revealing how complex these responses can be. For example, see Lazarus (1975) – 'The Self-Regulation of Emotion' – for an early example of this research; Lazarus and Folkman (1984) for 'coping' strategies; Cantor, Ziemke and Sparks (1984) for the effects of forewarning on emotional responses to horror; Sparks (1986, 1989, 1991) for cognitive and emotional responses to frightening films; Tamborini and Stiff (1987) for horror audiences; Tamborini, Stiff and Heidel (1990) for a model of empathy and emotional behaviour.

3.   See Gauntlett, 1995. *Moving Experiences: Understanding Television's Influences and Effects*, pp.17-37, 39-41. Gauntlett examines laboratory experiments, field experiments, longitudinal panel studies, amongst others, before making a claim for qualitative research into this area.

4.   Newson's report was widely discussed in all the papers. For example, see *Daily Mirror* (1 April 1994, p.1, 11), *The Times* (1 April 1994, p.3), *The Guardian* (1 April 1994, p.1, p.26) and coverage in the media from 1 April to 12 and 13 April 1994. This report was hugely influential in adding to the moral panic created by the 'video nasty' debate in the wake of the Jamie Bulger case. The fact that the report came out days before legislation regarding video viewing was added to the Criminal Justice Bill, and the fact that David Alton MP, the chief instigator in amending the Criminal Justice Act, commissioned the report, has been noted by critics of Newson's report. See Gauntlett (1995), Buckingham (1996a, 1996b).

5.   There was widespread coverage of the V-chip. It made the *News at Ten*, 18 March 1996, with an item that ran after coverage of the Government's decision to consider Britain's gun laws in the wake of the Dunblane tragedy. For press coverage see: *The Guardian*, 25 March 1996; *The Independent*, 19 March 1996, p.15 & 26 March 1996, p.2-3; *The Times*, 20 March 1996; *Broadcast*, 3 May 1996, p.16-19. See also Wark and Ball (1996) for a report in *The Sunday Times*, 23 June 1996, Focus section, p.12, into children viewing 'video nasties' and 'powerless parents' unable to stop such viewing. Needless to say the report is in favour of the V-chip.

cates children are as active in the decision-making processes associated with television viewing as adults.[6] If kids self-regulate, it is only natural to assume adults do the same.

The popular misconception of the 'passive' couch potato, when combined with the subject of violent movies, takes on sinister overtones. All too often, viewers of violent movies are demonized. As far back as 1925, Professor Cyril Burt was labelling people who like to watch 'crook-films' as 'defective', and in 1992 Michael Medved described those people who like to watch violent movies as 'drooling, hormone-addled, violence prone sub-literate adolescent males'.[7] It is this image of the moviegoer that is prevalent not just in the media but in certain political, academic and research circles. Hence, the Tory MP David Nicholson, in a recent Opinion Survey, asks the people of Taunton to tick whether they believe banning pornographic and violent videos will help tackle crime;[8] Cynthia A. Freeland (1995), in an essay on realist horror, refers to these films as targeting and victimizing viewers;[9] and Gerbner (1994, p.133) refers to violent representations as 'drenching every home with graphic scenes of expertly choreographed violence.'[10] Implicit in these reports of the insidious nature of violent movies is a dramatization of the kind of person who likes to watch these films as evil and depraved. It is no wonder Ben Elton (1996) satirized such moviegoers in his latest novel *Popcorn* – degenerate devotees of violent movies are all the rage.

This is how moral panics evolve. As Cohen and Young (1973) demonstrate in *The Manufacture of News: Deviance, Social Problems and the Mass Media*, 'moral panics' are engendered by media fantasies.[11] In this instance, the media fantasy of viewers of violent movies as impressionable and depraved is so potent, we are in danger of forgetting that violent movies are a popular leisure activity, and that many men and women choose this form of entertainment over other comparable activities. Indeed, they pay money to experience this entertainment.

It is time to redress the balance. The research undertaken in this book represents an attempt to indicate the positive responses to be gained from viewing violent movies and the results of this study are taken from recent empirical research, not media fantasies of 'depraved devotees' of violent movies.

---

6.   Buckingham (1996a), Barratt (1996), Gauntlett (1997) are examples of the most recent research in this field which indicates children develop coping strategies, and are active viewers from an early age. For a more comprehensive survey of this see Buckingham and Allerton (1996b).

7.   See Burt (1925), p.145, and Medved (1992), both cited in Kidd-Hewitt and Osborne (1995), 'Crime and the Media: a Criminological Perspective' p.6.

8.   This Opinion Survey was sent by David Nicholson MP (Tory) to people in Taunton in August 1996, and in question 4: 'Which one of the following would help most in tackling crime? (please tick)', a corresponding list (which includes capital punishment) contains point eight: 'Pornographic and violent videos banned'. This survey attempts to conflate pornography and violence which are two separate and complex issues, and, more worryingly, links violent videos with crime. The survey, sent in the run up to a general election, signals the way screen violence has become a political debate which has nothing to do with the actual content of the videos in question. Martin Barker, who noted similar political agendas in *Comics: Ideology, Power and the Critics*, will feel *déjà vu* I'm sure.

9.   See Freeland, C, 1995 'Realist Horror' p.136, in Freeland & Wartenburg, 1995. Freeland's article is both interesting and significant to the study of 'new brutalism' movies, and she has much to say in defence of these horror texts, but on the whole she is still sceptical of the pleasure to be gained from this form of entertainment. I would argue that this is an assumption not based on any empirical research, and as an assumption should be laid to rest.

10.   Cited in Gauntlett (1995), p.110.

11.   For examples of research into moral panics, see Cohen (1972), Cohen and Young (1973), Pearson (1983), Barker (1984), and Martin (1993).

There is a tradition of positive approaches to the subject of violent movies which is problematic and not to be confused with the approach adopted in this book. Positive approaches are usually referred to by the media as the 'liberal' approach, and Michael Winner is most often a representative of a 'liberal' who supports violent movies, arguing that films such as *Natural Born Killers* provide a 'safety valve' and offer 'vicarious enjoyment'.[12] Mannheim (1970) describes this approach as follows:

> The reader or watcher of brutal acts of violence, of sex orgies, or whatever outrageous material press and cinema may choose to place before them, far from wishing to do the same would rather *lean back happily and passively and let those actively engaged take his place*. Looked at this way, horror tales and crime films (are) not only not dangerous but positively useful as crime-preventing agencies. (my emphasis, p.601)

The problem with this approach is that there is no evidence to suggest a) viewers are passive, b) they are exclusively male, and c) that watching violent movies acts as a cathartic release. What there is evidence to suggest is that the viewer is active, male and female, and is able to differentiate between fictional violence and real violence in a way that indicates real violence is perceived as disturbing and abhorrent.[13] Recent studies undertaken by David Buckingham (1996) into children who watch 'video nasties', Schlesinger *et al* (1992) into women who watch violence on TV, and Morrison, MacGregor and Thorpe (1993) into methods of response to factual violence substantiate this claim.

Shocking Entertainment adds to this research and attempts to understand the process of viewing violence. The qualitative research conducted in this study demonstrates that active consumers of violent movies possess 'portfolios of interpretation'. This means that viewers utilize a number of reactive mechanisms in order to interpret fictional violence. These methods include:
• Anticipating violent images/scenes;
• Building character relationships;
• Self-censoring fictional violence;
• Testing boundaries.

Central to the process of viewing violence is the context of the viewing event as a social activity, where viewers can test boundaries safe in the knowledge that this is a fictional context, separate from their awareness of real violence in contemporary society. It is important to point out that boundary testing does not signify desensitization, but is the result of reactive mechanisms which con-

---

12.   There are numerous examples of this on TV and in the press. See Morrison, R, 1996. 'Who Supports Violent Films Now?' *The Times*, Saturday, 16 March, p.17. One recent example of the press using Michael Winner as an example of the 'liberal' approach is in *The Sunday Times*, 23 June 1996, p.12, where Winner is wheeled in to say that it's only natural to be interested in sex and violence.

13.   See Buckingham (1996a), Barratt (1996), Gauntlett (1995), Hagell & Newburn (1994), Gray, (1992), , Morrison (1993), Hargrave (1993) Docherty (1990) for research that indicates viewers are active and differentiate between real violence and fictional violence; and Schlesinger et al (1992), Oliver (1993), Sparks (1991), and Zillman et al (1986) for research that indicates men and women watch violence and horror. See in particular Hargrave (1993), pp.84-7 for discussion regarding methods of viewing factual violence. For theoretical approaches to this area, see Carroll (1990) and Clover (1992), who argue for complex and active methods of response to horror; see Smith (1995) and Bordwell (1985, 1989) for cognitive responses to film, and Carroll (1990) and Freeland and Wartenburg (1995) for philosophical approaches to film.

stitute methods of interpreting violence. By developing 'portfolios of interpretation', consumers of violent movies demonstrate how complex and dynamic the process of viewing violence can be.

Shocking Entertainment aims to explore the reactive mechanisms associated with viewing violent movies. By examining what moviegoers have to say about their viewing experiences, this book reveals that it is possible to construct a model of the viewing process, based on the notion of 'portfolios of interpretation'. The model of the viewing process and the notion of 'portfolios of interpretation' are discussed in depth in Chapter 9. The model indicates that contextual and individual factors form the viewing experience. The research in this book demonstrates it is possible to consider these factors and specify a 'value' for particular persons, or groups of people, based on the factors they utilize whilst viewing violence. Once this 'value' is recorded, it is possible to predict a reaction to, or diagnosis of violent movies.

It is this theory of 'portfolios of interpretation', and the subsequent model of the viewing process, which breaks the circular nature of the 'effects' debate so far. Rather than endlessly debating whether watching violent movies makes you violent, let us try to understand the complexity of response to the process of the viewing experience. Let us explore why violent movies are shocking and entertaining.

An overview of the study
This book begins with a detailed discussion of the research methods used in this study. Chapter 3 provides an overview of the target films and participants' perceptions of, and interests in, choosing to see these films. It is important to establish why participants are active consumers of violent movies, and how they differentiate between the target films as examples of 'new brutalism' and Hollywood action movies, such as the *Die Hard* series.

Chapter 4 looks at the activity of viewing violence, and considers how participants are aware of other moviegoers' response to violence as well as their own individual response. It is here participants discuss the range of physical and emotional responses to fictional violence they experience, and the significance of anticipation to the viewing process. Chapter 5 moves into a more detailed analysis of response to a scene from *Henry, Portrait of a Serial Killer* (John McNaughton, 1990), and participants reveal they do not identify with one character, but build character relationships using individual experience and imaginative hypothesizing. In this chapter, participants' response to violence can be seen as dynamic and fluid, and utilizing consumer choice, a theme taken up in later chapters in this study.

Chapter 6 provides the central focus of the study and is an in depth examination of participants' attitudes to thresholds and self-censorship, two factors which shape overall methods of viewing violence and highlight the significance of boundary testing, an activity which helps to explain why viewers choose to watch violent movies.

The remaining chapters, 7 and 8, consider the question of entertainment in relation to violent movies, and contribute a case study of viewer response to a scene from *Reservoir Dogs*, using the emergent themes detailed in the preceding chapters. The final chapter is an attempt to summarize the data and offer a model of the viewing process, based on the theory of portfolios of interpretation. It is this model which informs the policy recommendations to be found at the close of this book.

2
Designing the study

Locating the study

The object of researching response to viewing violence is to learn why people choose to watch violent movies and why they respond to violence in particular ways. This is a simple objective but nonetheless significant to any study which attempts to explore the process of viewing violence. Therefore, whilst at first I began my research into viewing violence by analyzing texts such as *Reservoir Dogs* or *Natural Born Killers*, and reading film theory, it soon became apparent that I was looking at the wrong material at the wrong stage in my research. What critics and theorists have to say about violent movies is certainly interesting, but does not notably contribute to answering the basic question: why do people choose to see violent movies?[1] Unless researchers actually talk to consumers of violent movies they will not be able to explain the appeal of such movies.

Consequently, this study tests certain hypotheses of my own about the process of viewing violence by conducting qualitative research into this area.[2] As is common in qualitative research, I soon discovered that the nature of participants' insights generated hypotheses as much as tested them, and in this respect the results of the qualitative research proved more rich and diverse than I could have hoped for.

As David Gauntlett (1995) has pointed out in his book *Moving Experiences: Understanding Television's Influences and Effects* listening to the audience goes beyond simple surveys and provides valuable research into the uses and interpretations of media consumption:

> The more sophisticated, qualitative…research which engages respondents with the focus of study, such as television depictions of violence,

---

1. For theoretical and textual analysis of violent movies see: Clover (1992), Creed (1993), Carroll (1990), Freeland (1995), Wood (1978) (1980), Grixti (1989) Sargeant (1995) amongst others. What each of these critics fails to address in sufficient detail is the significance of sociological research to theoretical approaches to violent movies. Buckingham (1996a) and Barratt (1996) also note this failing and call for an interdisciplinary approach which marries empirical research with theoretical reasoning. This approach would combine 'macro' and 'micro' levels of analysis [See Moores (1990)]. Martin Barker is currently using this approach to complete research in teenagers' response to action movies, and it is this approach I will myself adopt in the second stage of my research.

2. For discussion of qualitative research see Kirk and Miller (1986), Krueger (1988), Morgan (1988).

(is) more likely to reveal their actual feelings, concerns, interpretations and preferences about television output, than simple surveys which seek to keep television separate from the other questions in respondent's minds. (p.103)

Thus the models for this research are drawn from media and cultural studies, not from film theory, or psychological 'effects' research. Following in the footsteps of similar qualitative research studies into viewer response, such as *Video Playtime: The Gendering of a Leisure Technology*, Ann Gray (1992), *Women Viewing Violence*, Schlesinger, Dobash, Dobash & Weaver (1992), and *Moving Images: Understanding Children's Emotional Responses to Television*, David Buckingham (1996a), this study attempts to understand the complex and sophisticated response to viewing violence.

The dominant discourse of this study will be sociological; however, evidence from this research will inform and structure further studies concerned with the issue of violent movies. Following Buckingham (1996a), Barratt (1996) and Barker (1984, 1989) I believe that a combination of empirical research (the 'micro-level' of analysis) and theoretical inquiry (the 'macro-level' of analysis) provides the most productive means of researching the topic of violent movies.[3] Therefore, it is qualitative research which forms the basis of this book, but theoretical and textual analysis will aid an understanding of the process of viewing violence in later studies in this area.

Pilot studies

My research into viewing violence began as a series of pilot studies, using a combination of qualitative and quantitative research methods. Individual interviews and questionnaires were completed during a period of six months (January-June, 1995) and a total of 70 consumers of violent movies were either interviewed (20) or asked to fill in a questionnaire (50). Participants were recruited either by poster, direct address outside cinemas, or through the snowball technique. Whilst the results from these pilot studies were relevant to the question of why people choose to watch violent movies, both methods of questionnaire response and individual interviews were found lacking. For the purposes of this study, questionnaire response would only be useful if conducted on a large scale, and as this was not possible, it was thought better to turn to other more self-contained and manageable methods of collecting data. What is more, the purpose of this study is to explore the complex and sophisticated response to viewing violence, not attempt to survey a cross section of the general public on their viewing tastes. Individual interviews proved a more successful method; however they lacked an interaction of ideas, and over time I came to recognize this interaction is necessary to understanding the process of viewing violence, an activity which is more social than individual.[4]

Consequently, I chose to conduct self-contained focus groups, as the advantage of focus groups is that they provide an opportunity to collect data from

---

3.   See Moores (1993, p.140) cited in Barratt (1996, p.64).

4.   Other research in media studies confirms this. Recent ethnographic work by Gray (1992), Gillespie (1995), Palmer (1986), and Gauntlett (1997) explores media texts and social relations as a primary focus of research.

group interaction (See Morgan [1988], Krueger [1988], Greenbaum [1987]).[5] This group interaction takes the basis of lively and informal conversation which explores specific topics and reveals cognitive processes at work. It is this ability to register cognitive processes and generate hypotheses which makes focus groups the most productive method of collecting data for this research. As David L. Morgan states in *Focus Groups as Qualitative Research* (1988, p.25): 'Focus groups are useful when it comes to investigating *what* participants think, but they excel at uncovering *why* participants think as they do'.

Therefore, the aim of this study is not to reach statistical conclusions about who watches violent movies but to test and to develop my own hypotheses regarding the process of viewing violence. A triangulation of methods have been used to design this study; this is a system of using a number of sources, encouraged within the sociological field.[6] These methods are: individual interviews; questionnaires; and focused group discussions. However, self-contained focus groups form the primary method of data analysis in the study as a whole. The term 'self-contained' signifies that the results of these focus groups can stand on their own; however, this qualitative data can also be incorporated into a larger body of research if and when this should be undertaken.

Designing the focus groups

This study focuses on active consumers of violent movies and explores the reactive mechanisms of thresholds and self-censorship and the issue of gender in relation to the viewing process. The movies considered in the focus groups are films which have been given a theatrical 18 Certificate release, and (in all but one case[7]) are available on video, but have not been screened on terrestrial television.[8] These films are therefore available but have to be actively sought by consumers and either seen at the cinema and/or in the home environment.

'New brutalism' and films used in the study

Eight movies were chosen as exemplifying societal/cultural consensus of extremely violent films, an important consideration when considering the role of boundary testing, and the reactive mechanisms of thresholds and self-censorship, when viewing violence. These films are:

---

5. For discussion of qualitative research and focus groups see, Denzin (1970), Giddens (1976), Goldman and McDonald (1987), Hughes (1990), Greenbaum (1987), May 1993) amongst others.

6. See Fielding and Fielding (1986) and Denzin (1970).

7. *Natural Born Killers* (Oliver Stone, 1994) is still awaiting a video release, despite the fact the BBFC has passed this film for its video certificate. After the Dunblane massacre in March 1996, Warner Brothers, the producers of this film, withdrew the release date, claiming it would not be appropriate to release the film in the light of the Dunblane massacre. See Wintour and Bunting (1996), *The Guardian*, Thursday 14 March 1996. This decision places *Natural Born Killers* in a problematic position which in many ways links it to the cause and effect of screen violence. Warner Brothers are signalling their extreme anxiety in relation to the video release of this film, by withholding its release date, and conferring with David Alton, the Liberal Democrat MP who wishes to see this film banned.

8. The BBC hold the rights to show *Natural Born Killers* on terrestrial television, but claim they will not screen this film before 1998, and indeed it may never be shown. See Culf, 1996, *The Guardian*, Wednesday 27 March 1996, p.7. Channel Four hold the rights to show *Reservoir Dogs*, but as yet have not announced any plans to do so due to the present climate which would make the broadcasting of such a notoriously violent film difficult. See Goodwin, 1994, 'You've Been Framed', *Broadcast*, 22 April, p.15.

Table 1: Target Films

Film	Director	Year
Reservoir Dogs	Quentin Tarantino	1992
Pulp Fiction	Quentin Tarantino	1994
True Romance	Tony Scott	1993
Natural Born Killers	Oliver Stone	1994
Man Bites Dog	Belvaux, Bonzel, Poelvoorde	1992
Henry, Portrait of a Serial Killer	John McNaughton	1990 (Prod. 1986)
Bad Lieutenant	Abel Ferrara	1992
Killing Zoe	Roger Avary	1994

These films were released in Britain during 1990 to 1995, however, it was the release of *Reservoir Dogs* (Tarantino, 1992) which attracted media interest in what began to be described as a 'new wave' of violent movies. This prompted the media to discuss the target films as extreme, and uncompromising in their depictions of violence on screen. When *Reservoir Dogs* was released in the UK in January 1993, journalists and film critics highlighted Tarantino's 'cinema of viscera'.[9] Alexander Walker, in the *Evening Standard*, ran an interview with Tarantino, titled: 'Shooting the Dogs of Gore';[10] whilst Shaun Usher, in the *Daily Mail*, wrote a review of *Reservoir Dogs* titled: 'Deadly Dogs Unleash a Whirlwind of Violence'.[11]

Consequently, it is the release of Tarantino's first film and the popularity of Tarantino's 'cinema of viscera' (Dargis, 1994) which fuelled debate regarding contemporary violent movies. Quentin Tarantino is involved as director, writer or producer in five out of the eight target films: he wrote and directed *Reservoir Dogs* and *Pulp Fiction*; he wrote the screenplay for True Romance; he wrote the original script, and subsequent story for *Natural Born Killers*; and he executive produced *Killing Zoe*. Not surprisingly, it is his reputation as 'The Gun Guy' which has affected societal/cultural consensus of these films. Ephraim Katz describes Tarantino as a film maker of 'blistering, uncompromising dramatic fare' (1992, p.1329); the *Guardian Weekend* magazine describes Tarantino as 'a connoisseur of cruelty' (Sigal, 1993, p.24), whilst Quentin Tarantino tells Geoff Andrew (1994, p.26) in *Time Out*: 'I don't think you can go too far with violence if what you are doing is right for the movie. What's too far?'

With regard to the three target films Tarantino is not involved with, each of these movies have been marketed as extreme and disturbing. Derek Malcolm (1993a) describes *Man Bites Dog* as follows: 'it makes *Reservoir Dogs* look like muzzled mongrels', a quote displayed on the video cover of this film. Similarly the video cover for *Henry, Portrait of a Serial Killer*, which was released not long after *Reservoir Dogs* in 1993, carries the warning: 'This film contains scenes which may be disturbing to some viewers' (Electric Pictures, 1993). *Bad Lieutenant* is described by Jonathan Romney (1993, p.34) as a 'One way ticket to hell', with even the *Sun* referring to the movie and it's star (Harvey Keitel), who also appears in *Reservoir Dogs*, as 'Gore Blimey Keitel's Back.'[12]

9.   Manohla Dargis, 'Pulp Instincts' in *Sight and Sound*, Vol.4, Issue 5, May 1994, p.6.

10.   Walker, 1992. 'Shooting the Dogs of Gore' in the *Evening Standard*, 5 November 1992, pp.43-44.

11.   Usher, S, 1992. 'Deadly Dogs Unleash a Whirlwind of Violence' in the *Daily Mail*. 22 December 1992, p.26.

12.   Cox, Peter, 1993. 'Gore Blimey Keitel's Back' in the *Sun*. 19 February 1993, p.19. The same week *Bad Lieutenant* was released in the UK, *Mean Streets* (Martin Scorsese, 1993) was re-released at the

Quite why the *Sun* could refer to Keitel in such a way must be attributed to the cluster of violent movies released at the start of 1993. A week after the UK release date of *Reservoir Dogs* (January 8th 1993), *Man Bites Dog* was released, and only a few weeks after that *Bad Lieutenant* gained its theatrical release (19th February 1993).[13] This prompted journalists to speak of a 'new wave' of visceral films which fuelled the debate about screen violence. Hence, the *Daily Telegraph* ran an article, 'Are These Films Too Violent?', where it interviewed James Ferman of the British Board of Film Classification and asked whether he could be held responsible for releasing such a wave of violence.[14] Similarly, an article by B. Ruby Rich in *Sight and Sound* comments on the intense and individualised violence which is a hallmark of these films: she describes these movies as a 'wave of neo-violence' (Rich, 1992, p.5) specific to the 1990s. Another journalist, Jim Shelley (1993a, p.7, 1993b, p.12), refers collectively to these films as 'heralding the arrival of "the new brutalism"' no less than twice in two separate articles early in 1993.

It is because of the notoriety of these films as uncompromising violent movies that I have chosen to use the term 'new brutalism' to differentiate these films from other movies of similar content.[15] What these movies share, in terms of content, is a preoccupation with violence towards the individual, as opposed to the state, and, in terms of style, the use of realism when representing violence. These eight films were chosen to represent a current cultural trend in violent movies. There were many films that could have been added to the list, but it was these eight that served the purpose of prompting participants to discuss why they choose to watch violent movies.

'Violent movies' and 'desensitisation'

A note on the terms 'violence' and 'desensitisation' is applicable here. The term 'violent movies' is used to refer to societal/cultural consensus of the target films. Care was taken in the focus groups not to introduce the terms 'violent movies' or 'desensitisation' until participants had done so of their own accord, less an air of condemnation derived from the term 'violence' coupled with 'desensitisation' descend onto the focus group discussions before they had even begun. As societal/cultural consensus of the target films and consumers of these films is so overwhelmingly negative (see the above section, and Chapter 1 for examples of this), it was only practical to allow participants to introduce the terms of reference themselves, as it would not do for the moderator to appear anything other than neutral in this regard.

The term 'violent movies' with reference to the target films did not prove problematic within the discussion groups. Participants appeared comfortable using this term, and if they wished to differentiate between different types of

---

cinema. As Harvey Keitel stars in both films, and was also in *Reservoir Dogs*, only released a month before, this no doubt prompted the *Sun* to comment on his appearance, though why "gore" is mentioned can only be attributed to the 'New Violence' current in the press at the start of 1993.

13. Soon to follow in 1993 was the re-release of *Mean Streets* (Martin Scorsese, 1973), and the UK release of *Hard Boiled* (John Woo), the Australian film *Romper Stomper*, and the video release of *Henry, Portrait of a Serial Killer*. All referred to in Guttridge (1993, p.18).

14. Guttridge, Peter, 1993. 'Are These Films Too Violent?' in the *Daily Telegraph*. 22 January 1993, p.18.

15. As far as I can tell, the term originates from Jim Shelley who is the only journalist I have found who refers to these films as "the new Brutalism" in two articles at the start of 1993. See Shelley (1993a, p.7, 1993b, p.12). David Gauntlett (1995, p.5) also uses this term when discussing *Reservoir Dogs*, and *Henry, Portrait of a Serial Killer*.

fictional violence they did so of their own accord. As Chapter 7, 'The Question of Entertainment', will indicate, when participants wished to question, or qualify a term of reference used in the discussion groups, they did so in no uncertain terms.

The term 'desensitization' was used on occasion by participants, yet those few participants who chose to use this term were careful to qualify what they felt it signified to them and their personal experience of viewing violence. Chapter 6, 'Thresholds and Self-Censorship', considers the reactive mechanisms common to participants' viewing experience, and the latter half of this chapter deals in some detail with the concept of boundary testing, which is not aligned with the notion of 'desensitization', as used by the media, but is defined as a term of reference in its own right, specific to particular types of leisure activities, in this instance screen entertainment. Chapter 7, 'The Question of Entertainment', and Chapter 8, 'Reservoir Dogs: A Case Study', examine the significance of boundary testing within specific contexts, and here the term 'desensitization', when used by participants, is qualified and interpreted as something quite separate from media definitions of 'desensitization' as an abhorrent and socially unacceptable form of response. Here, it is clear 'desensitization' is being re-defined by participants, and it is their examination of this phrase which indicates that a separate term of reference should be used in order to differentiate between 'desensitization', as used by the media, and boundary testing, as a means of interpreting violence.[16]

Consequently, the term 'violent movies', and other related terms, such as 'viewing violence', have been adopted in this study in order to accurately reflect the content of the discussion groups and participants' response to the target films. In contrast, the term 'desensitization' has not been adopted in this study, and the term 'boundary testing' has been employed in order to accurately reflect participants' response to the viewing experience. However, as I shall discuss in Chapter 9, 'Summary and Conclusion', this does not mean that other terms of reference for the subject of violent movies and the issue of desensitization would not be welcomed. As other writers and researchers, such as Martin Barker (1984), have pointed out, more detailed terms of reference to violent movies, for example in relation to genre, only serve to open up debate regarding the issue of violence, something much needed in our present climate of hostility towards violent movies. The aim of this study is to facilitate a more open forum for debate, and encourage a variety of responses to the issue of violence.

Criteria and recruitment

The criteria for selecting participants for the focus group discussions was kept very simple. The criteria were:
• Participants must be over 18 years old;
• Participants must have seen three or more films on the target list;
• Participants must not be engaged in any research in this field.

---

16. There have been a number of studies into 'the desensitization hypothesis', and David Gauntlett (1995) discusses these in *Moving Experiences* (pp.39-40). As Gauntlett points out, although some studies claim to find examples of 'desensitized' viewers (see Van Evra [1990, pp.96-97]), this does not necessarily suggest viewers are numb to real violence, only more used to fictional representations of violence. In any case, research by Belson (1978) and Hagell and Newburn (1994) find no evidence to support 'the desensitization hypothesis'.

These straightforward criteria enabled me to recruit current consumers of violent movies who did not have a clear agenda, but who did have an active interest in the research subject.

Male and female participants were recruited equally in order to ensure that all male, all female and mixed gender focus groups contained a balanced mix of participants. The decision to ensure this balance of focus groups reflects the nature of this study which is to examine why people watch violent movies: 'people' includes male and female consumers, a fact often overlooked when considering the role of the consumer and violent movies. It is one concern of this study to examine whether there is any noticeable difference between the way men and women view violence.[17]

Recruitment was conducted using the snowball technique, with follow up phone calls and letters explaining the nature of the focused discussions. This proved to be time-consuming and difficult to achieve, but it did produce a collection of participants who were not specifically self-selective, and who, although interested in the research subject, would not go out of their way to openly discuss their opinions. Telephone calls helped to select participants who fitted this criteria. There were particular problems recruiting female consumers of violent movies, who, although available in theory, were difficult to persuade to join the discussions. Many women would only come to single sex discussions, and if they could not make the suggested dates, were lost as potential participants. Similar difficulties did not occur when recruiting male participants, who exhibited a confidence in choosing to become part of the focus groups which many female participants lacked. The end result reveals a slight gender difference in recruitment, with 20 male participants and 16 female participants contributing to the discussions.

Background characteristics of participants

The sample used in this research does not constitute a representative survey, and consequently macro-sociological patterns, such as class, or ethnicity (with the exception of gender, see this chapter, 'Criteria and Recruitment'), do not feature as part of this research. However, certain basic demographic data were collected during the focus group discussions and are documented here as a source of information to be used in future research in this area.

The Cinema Advertising Association undertakes film profiles which are representative samples of the British population and serve to highlight such macro-sociological patterns as age, gender and the social background of moviegoers. Tables 2a, 2b, and 2c reveal that participants who took part in the focus groups share similar macro-sociological patterns to those outlined in the CAA's representative sample. For example, in the CAA Film Profile the average age of moviegoers who went to see *Pulp Fiction* is between 20 and 34, which corresponds with the average age of those participants in the focus groups who went to see *Pulp Fiction* (See Table 2c). Similarly, the CAA Film Profile reveals that although there is some difference in figures between the numbers of male and female participants who went to see this film (65 per cent and 35 per cent respectively) the number of female moviegoers still represents a substantial amount (see Table 2a). Although the number of female participants in the focus groups who saw this film is higher that the CAA sur-

---

17. For discussion of gendered response to violent movies in sociological research see, Buckingham (1996a), Schlesinger et al (1992), Gunter and Wober (1988), Docherty (1990).

vey, this cross reference still indicates that female consumers of violent movies are a force to be reckoned with. Where relevant, cross references will be made between the Cinema Advertising Association's representative sample, and my own breakdown of the background characteristics of participants in this study.

Table 2a: CAA Film Profiles – Gender

Film	Male	Female	Total
Reservoir Dogs	62%	38%	1,344,000
Pulp Fiction	65%	35%	4,330,000
True Romance	72%	28%	343,000
Natural Born Killers	71%	29%	1,846,000
Man Bites Dog	46%	54%	286,000
Killing Zoe	66%	34%	250,000

Figures supplied by Cinema Advertising Association, August, 1996. No figures for Henry, Portrait of a Serial Killer or Bad Lieutenant.

Table 2b: CAA Film Profile – Class[18]

Film	ABC1	C2DE	Total
Reservoir Dogs	56%	44%	1,344,000
Pulp Fiction	60%	40%	4,330,000
True Romance	71%	29%	343,000
Natural Born Killers	57%	43%	1,846,000
Man Bites Dog	56%	44%	286,000
Killing Zoe	75%	26%	250,000

Figures supplied by Cinema Advertising Association, August, 1996. No figures for Henry, Portrait of a Serial Killer or Bad Lieutenant.

Table 2c: CAA Film Profiles – Age

Film	18-19	20-24	25-34	35-44	45+	Total
R D	14%	53%	18%	6%	10%	1,344,000
PF	12%	31%	34%	13%	10%	4,330,000
TR	35%	19%	32%	6%	7%	343,000
NBK	15%	40%	26%	12%	7%	1,846,000
MBD	6%	58%	29%	0%	8%	286,000
KZ	20%	40%	41%	0%	0%	250,000

Figures supplied by Cinema Advertising Association, August, 1996. No figures for Henry, Portrait of a Serial Killer or Bad Lieutenant.

Participants were asked to fill in a short registration form (see Appendix 3). Information given in these registration forms provides a useful indicator of participants' age; ethnic background; education; cinemas frequented; and magazines/newspapers most often read. Other information regarding the target films has been used in the main body of this study and will not be repeated here.

Participants were aged between 18 and 50. The most common age bracket was between 18-30, with 10 participants aged between 18-20, and 16

---

18.   The Cinema Advertising Association uses the following codes to represent class structures: A = Upper Middle Class; B = Middle Class; C1 = Lower Middle Class; C2 = Skilled Working Class; D = Working Class; E = Lowest Level of Subsistence. The CAA Film Profile provides figures for ABC1 and C2DE.

participants aged between 20-30, making a total of 26 participants aged 30 or under taking part in the discussions. Only 10 participants were over 30, and only one out of that figure was over 40. This corresponds with those figures supplied by the CAA Film Profile which indicates that the average age of moviegoers for the target films is 18-34 (see Table 2c for cross reference). The vast proportion of participants were British (33), with only 3 participants being of a different ethnic origin (1 Indian, 1 Australian, 1 Chinese).[19] All participants were educated to GCSE level/A level standard, with 21 participants having finished a technical or vocational course or part of a university course and three participants who had completed a post graduate course. Although there is no breakdown of figures for the education of moviegoers in the CAA Profile of the target films, Table 2b reveals that the target films are more popular with the ABC1 bracket, which includes middle class workers, than the C2DE bracket, which includes the working class. Whilst this is not offered as substitute information, the class breakdown does offer some indication that the target films are more popular with middle class (educated) moviegoers, although some films, such as *Reservoir Dogs*, attract similar figures from both social brackets.

Response to the 'cinemas most frequented' question on the registration form was varied, and indicates participants use their local cinemas as frequently, if not more than West End cinemas. There was no common cinema mentioned, but reference to various local and independent cinemas in the London area. Response to which newspapers/ magazines participants read reveals participants read a variety of broadsheet newspapers and magazines, the most common being the *Guardian, Empire, The Face* and *Time Out*. For a breakdown of these reading figures see Table 2: Reading Figures for Popular Newspapers/Magazines in Chapter 3, 'Consumer Choice and Violent Movies'.

Conducting the focus groups
A pilot focus group was conducted in order to test the suitability of questions and viewing material during the discussion period and to give an indication of time requirements and group interaction. Participants in the pilot study were from Roehampton Institute London.

A series of six focus groups were conducted at The Green Door Cafe in London, between November to December 1995. Numbers of the focus groups were kept relatively small, between 4-6, although one focus group did include seven participants. The reason why the focus groups contained small numbers was to encourage group interaction and in-depth discussion of the process of viewing violence. Small groups fostered an intimate atmosphere, and enabled all participants to reflect and consider their complex and sophisticated response to violent movies.

The discussions took place on Saturday afternoons in a restaurant hired solely for the purposes of this study, and this location was a deliberate choice because I felt it was important to provide a neutral, safe environment for participants who were being asked to consider a sensitive issue, an issue where the concept of safety is very important (see Chapter 7, section 2, 'The Safety of

---

19. The terms 'Indian', 'Australian', and 'Chinese' were used by participants themselves when filling in the ethnic origin section in the registration form for focus group participants.

Cinema' for further discussion). Wine, soft drinks and light refreshments were made available, and once again, the decision to provide alcohol was designed in order to relax participants and foster a more social environment. Offering wine in a restaurant seemed a logical step to take.

The format for the focus group discussions was standardized, although, where appropriate, allowance was made for specific issues raised by participants in a given group. Discussion was opened with a request for brief biographical information, and participants were invited to offer their opinions concerning the target films. Initial reactions were followed by a more focused discussion guided by a series of questions posed by myself, acting as moderator (see Appendix I).

Three cues were used: a list of target films (see Appendix II), a scene from the film *Reservoir Dogs*, and a scene from the film *Henry, Portrait of a Serial Killer*. Both film clips were shown during the discussion, and timed to coincide with specific questions related to these two scenes. The two scenes chosen were: the eye-stabbing scene from *Henry, Portrait of a Serial Killer* directed by John McNaughton, 1990 (produced 1986) and the ear-amputation scene from the film *Reservoir Dogs* directed by Quentin Tarantino, 1992. The eye-stabbing scene was chosen as an example of extreme violence which challenges notions of characterization and would be useful as a visual prompt when considering the issue of characterization in violent movies; the ear-amputation scene was chosen because it exemplifies an infamous scene of extreme violence which challenges notions of acceptability and therefore proves a useful visual prompt when discussing the issue of boundary testing, and the reactive mechanisms of thresholds and self-censorship.

The discussions lasted two and a quarter hours. A short break occurred after the screening of the eye-stabbing scene from *Henry, Portrait of a Serial Killer*, approximately half way through the discussion, and once again this was designed to encourage participants to relax and interact with one another.

The question of interaction is of particular significance to this study. It was noted by myself and the assistant moderator that male participants were less likely to express their thoughts and explore the process of viewing violence than female participants. In male-only focus groups, stiff body movements, and an unwillingness to expand on responses to questions posed by the moderator meant that a great deal of prompting and follow up questions were needed to ensure group discussion ran smoothly. In contrast, female-only focus groups positively thrived on group interaction, and very little follow up questions were needed to ensure group discussion was relaxed and lively.[20]

Male-only focus groups proved more difficult to run. A marked difference could be seen when mixed gender groups took place and this was because the presence of female participants visibly relaxed those male participants present. However, as the focus groups progressed it became easier to break down initial barriers, and, through experience and observation, provide as open an atmosphere as possible in all focus groups. The presence of a male assistant moderator was a significant means of relaxing male participants and

---

20. The fact that I was a female moderator undoubtedly influenced participants' interaction in the focus group discussions to some degree. However, the presence of a male assistant moderator went some way towards achieving a balance of gender in this regard. For discussion of this issue, see Padfield and Procter (1996), Bell, Caplan and Karim (1993), Finch (1993), McKee and O'Brien (1983).

encouraging informal discussion.[21] During the breaks, in particular, it was noticed that male participants were naturally drawn to the assistant moderator to make casual conversation, and this proved important in breaking down barriers when discussing the reactive mechanisms of thresholds and self-censorship, which occurred directly after the break.

Data collection instruments and analysis

As moderator, I adopted a neutral role and posed the same questions in each group to ensure a systematic protocol. Every necessary step was taken to ensure reliability and validity; the same questions were asked in the same order, the same cues were used at the same time in the discussion, and the same location was used each week. Three data collection points were used in an attempt to triangulate the data. These data collection points were:

• The moderator;
• The assistant moderator;
• Audio recording equipment.

The data collection points aided an important validity check; by the fourth focus group, material was found to be substantially repeated by participants, and focus groups 5 and 6 served to document the reliability of participants' observations over a period of time.

Each focus group was fully transcribed. Preliminary readings of transcripts assessed emergent themes and useful categories for analysis. Report writing proved a useful preliminary stage for analysis of the data, and a short report was made after each focus group was conducted. Similarly, discussions with my research supervisors and the assistant moderator aided the development of interpretation and analysis of the transcripts. A systematic approach to the presentation of themes has been adopted and illustrative quotes have been chosen as those best served to represent the dominant themes arising from the focus groups.

Participants have not been identified as male or female unless the data analysis is directly concerned with gender issues. Illustrative quotes are attributed to individual participants but the code of reference is anonymous, detailing the number of the group member in each focus group, and the number of which focus group this participant attended, for example (Participant 1 – FG1). The reason for this anonymity is to best represent group comments as a whole and not to single out individual participants unless a specific point is made regarding an individual's response. The issue of gender is only significant at certain stages in the data analysis; to indicate the gender of every illustrative quote would be to highlight this issue unnecessarily, and in certain instances bias the study towards the issue of gender when the first object of this study is to examine the process of viewing violence.

---

21. See Padfield and Procter (1996), Bell, Caplan and Karim (1993), Finch (1993), McKee and O'Brien (1983) for discussion of the effect of researchers' gender on the interview process.

3

Consumer choice and violent movies

Hype, scandal and cultural cachet

There are a number of reasons why participants choose to see the target films: media hype; peer pressure; advertising; personal preference for specific directors or actors; personal experience: these are all factors which influence participants to watch, or not watch violent movies.

The number of target films participants have seen is indicated in Table 3. Figures reveal *Pulp Fiction, Reservoir Dogs, True Romance* and *Natural Born Killers* (in that order) are the most popular films to have been seen by participants, and *Bad Lieutenant, Man Bites Dog, Henry, Portrait of a Serial Killer,* and *Killing Zoe* (in that order) are the least popular films to have been seen by participants. These figures correlate with the official UK box office grosses for 1996 (see Table 4). The most popular target films with participants are also the most popular target films at the cinema, with a film such as *Pulp Fiction* grossing over £10,000,000 at the box office, while a film such as *Man Bites Dog* grossed just over £73,000 (*Screen International,* 1996). There is a slight difference in figures, with *True Romance* scoring higher with participants than at the box office, and *Killing Zoe* scoring lower with participants than at the box office, but over all it can be seen that participants' viewing figures for the target films correspond with the official UK box office figures for the target films. For a more detailed breakdown of participants' cinema and video viewing figures, see Chapter 6, 'Thresholds and Self-Censorship', Tables 7 and 8.

Table 3: Viewing Figures for Target Films

Film	Male	Female	Total
Reservoir Dogs	20	16	36
Pulp Fiction	20	16	36
True Romance	15	14	29
Natural Born Killers	10	9	19
Man Bites Dog	9	6	15
Henry, Portrait of...	8	6	14
Bad Lieutenant	11	5	16
Killing Zoe	6	3	9

Table 4: UK Box Office Grosses, 1996

Film	Box Office Figures
Reservoir Dogs	£ 5,900,719
Pulp Fiction	£10,446,312
True Romance	£ 2,179,160
Natural Born Killers	£ 4,849,685
Man Bites Dog	£ 73,697
Henry, Portrait of...	£ 72,598
Bad Lieutenant	£ 373,634
Killing Zoe	£ 465,997

Figures supplied by Screen International

Group members commented on media hype and peer pressure as determining factors in their choice of movie. The most popular magazines and newspapers cited by participants are the *Guardian, Empire, The Face, Time Out, The Independent, The Times, New Musical Express* (see Table 5). This indicates participants read the broadsheet papers and popular cultural magazines, in particular, the *Guardian* and *Empire,* and in doing so are kept in touch with current movie news and movie hype.

Table 5: Reading figures for popular newspapers/magazines

Title	Male	Female	Total
Empire	6	3	9
The Face	2	4	6
The Guardian	8	8	16
The Independent	2	3	5
New Musical Express	3	2	5
Time Out	4	2	6
The Times	3	2	5

For some, media hype discouraged participants from seeing specific films, such as *Natural Born Killers,* and for others it was the very intensity of media hype that ensured they would be drawn to see certain films. Participants explain their reaction:

> These films have a particular reputation and I think I've got to see them and form my own opinions. If there is a controversy then I'll make a special effort to watch the film and see what it's all about. (Participant 3 – FG4)

> Finding out about these films isn't too hard because any violent film gets a lot of publicity. If a film is getting a lot of publicity then I'll try and make an effort to see it; if it's making that much of a difference to other people it must be worth seeing. (Participant 4 – FG6)

> You hear all these rumours and scandals about these films and you think, what's the fuss all about? You go and see the films just to find out whether it's worth all the hype and bullshit. (Participant 3 – FG6)

It is because the target films attract a specific kind of publicity that participants are drawn to view a film in order to test their own response to that of the media. Therefore, in the case of a movie such as *Reservoir Dogs* (1992) its cinematic release attracted controversial publicity, and consequently the film was subject to rumours and scandal, not just in the media but as a cultural phenomenon in itself (see Chapter 8, '*Reservoir Dogs*, a Case Study' for further discussion). Many participants claimed they were drawn to see this film precisely because they wished to enter the cultural debate, and judge whether the controversy was justified.

Many participants linked media hype with peer pressure. Two group members comment on this:

> I'm swayed by media hype. Films like *Reservoir Dogs*, everyone's talking about it, and if you haven't seen it you're not in the gang. (Participant 2 – FG4)

> One reason I didn't see *Reservoir Dogs* was because people had said they'd seen it and even though they said it was a good film, for some reason I didn't want to go and see it because I knew it was violent. I think probably this was because it was one of the first films of that genre that was very publicly known, very much talked about and for that reason I didn't want to see it. When I did, I thought it was a great film. (Participant 5 – FG3)

Both participants cite media hype as a significant factor in relation to peer pressure. In the first example, this participant claims he feels left out, not part of the gang who have seen the movie, and his desire to be part of this gang is such that he chooses to see the film. The second participant cites an opposite reaction. It is because the film has attracted so much interest that she resists becoming part of the phenomena of *Reservoir Dogs*. She perceives this film as the start of the 'new brutalism' movies to appear at the cinema in 1992, and avoids the film because it has attracted controversy for its violent representations.

Closely linked to the factors of media hype and peer pressure is the role of advertising in the publicity and distribution of the target films. Participants cited trailers and adverts as influential, but part of the media hype and peer pressure related to a particular film. They did not single out any advert, trailer or piece of advertising merchandise as the sole reason why they chose to see one of the target films. It is an accumulation of factors rather than one reason alone which influences consumer choice.

Some participants cited personal preference for specific directors and actors as a contributing factor to their decision-making process. Three participants discuss this:

> I was interested to see John Travolta in *Pulp Fiction* because he's a really good actor. (Participant 2 – FG6)

> I wouldn't say I'm a Tarantino fan but his films interest me, I enjoy the fast pace, there is always something there. After *Reservoir Dogs* I got interested in his films and now I watch most of them. (Participant 1 – FG6)

> The actors make a difference. I can't stand Juliette Lewis and she put me off watching *Natural Born Killers*. (Participant 5 – FG3)

Such comments highlight the significance of personal preferences and consumer choice. Both these factors are not limited to discussion of actors or directors but can be expanded to include personal experience and preference for types of movies and types of violence. For example, some participants, in particular women, claimed their decision-making process could be affected adversely if a film contained specific scenes or levels of violence they personally found disturbing. Two female participants explain:

> Really violent films aren't my cup of tea, so I wouldn't choose to go and see one unless I knew exactly what was in it and how violent it was. Friends tell me the plot and how disgustingly violent it is and I'll go and see it if it's not too violent. (Participant 2 – FG3)

> It's a matter of personal experience. If I know a film has a rape scene in it, it has a very different effect on me whether I want to watch it or not, regardless of whether its been reviewed or recommended. I don't like violence towards females, it's very personal, I mean I just don't like it. (Participant 5 – FG3)

Here, both participants identify thresholds when viewing violence and choose to watch/not watch a film according to these thresholds which are based on personal experience and preferences. This is of interest later when the reactive mechanisms of thresholds and self-censorship are shown to be integral to the process of viewing violence. Self-censorship in this instance highlights consumer choice and the question of entertainment: excessive violence and representations of rape are not considered entertaining or desirable for these participants.

Other participants, in particular men, choose to watch the target films in order to monitor their response to viewing violence. One group member comments:

> I'm interested in my reactions to violent films because I think I don't like them. So, I put myself through it to see if I can tolerate the violence. It's a purposeful position. I adopt this kind of bunker mentality, like I'm steeling myself to not be shocked. (Participant 1 – FG4)

This illustration serves to highlight the preparation and conscious desire of certain male participants to not be shocked by the violent content in the target films. This is of interest when male attitudes to thresholds and self-censorship are analyzed in later chapters. Here, it indicates that the concept of monitoring response is one factor that influences male participants to choose to view the target films.

Whilst it may appear gender affects the decision-making process, in relation to the violent content of a film, there are complex and subtle reasons why participants choose to view the target films and in these instances the issue of gender is not straightforward or easy to define. For example, one female participant explains:

> I thought I was a sensitive person who didn't like violent films. I shied away from them. I thought they were morally wrong. And then you go through a stage where all your boundaries just dissolve and you don't know where the hell you are, and you feel liberated at the same time. I think film is a good medium for doing that because it is so

realistic, it enables you to use your brain and feel immediate catharsis. It's very therapeutic. (Participant 2 – FG5)

When she ended a five year relationship, this participant discovered another friend in a similar position and both women chose to see violent movies as a form of 'immediate catharsis', spending six months choosing to see violent films above any other genre. This participant claims she considered herself as going against type and gaining satisfaction from this; using the representations of violence as a safe way of experiencing anger and revenge. She views violent films as a form of therapy, and now considers herself an active consumer of violent films.

Whilst, on the one hand, this participant could be perceived as going against gender type when choosing to view violent movies, she could also be reacting against the concept that violent movies are 'morally wrong'. Her sense of catharsis could be attributed to her experience that violent movies can be liberating and that as a woman she can enjoy violent films, a possibility she did not consider before her relationship ended.

Reference to Table 3 and the viewing figures for the target films reveals a small difference between male and female participants' viewing figures. For example, 20 male and 16 female participants have seen *Reservoir Dogs* and *Pulp Fiction*; 15 male and 14 female participants have seen True Romance; 9 male and 6 female participants have seen *Man Bites Dog*. However, reference to Table 2a (see Chapter 2, 'Designing the Study') and the Cinema Advertising Association's Film Profile of the target films reveals that there are more significant differences between male and female viewing figures for the target films in this survey. For example, 65 per cent (male) and 35 per cent (female) chose to see *Pulp Fiction* in the CAA Film Profile. Therefore, whilst the figures in Table 2a and Table 3 do indicate gender difference in viewing habits, Table 3 places this difference as less notable than Table 2a. As Table 2a represents a large, representative sample it is probably wise to take these figures as more representative of the gender orientation of moviegoers of the target films. However, the difference in figures may suggest that gender differences in viewing habits should be investigated further before generalisations are made. The fact that 35 per cent of the representative sample in the CAA Film Profile were women who chose to see *Pulp Fiction*, and 54 per cent (female) chose to see *Man Bites Dog*, does indicate many women are choosing to see violent movies, something rarely mentioned by the media when discussing this issue.

What has become apparent in all focus groups is that *Reservoir Dogs* and *Pulp Fiction* are two films participants consider necessary to see: in Table 3 viewing figures for these target films reveal each movie has been seen by all participants, and Table 4 reveals how popular both these films were (and still are) at the box office. The films are signs of social and cultural success, and there is a cachet in being part of such cultural events, part of a zeitgeist. None of the other target films can compete in terms of popularity and cultural significance. As one participant says: 'How can you go to a dinner party if you haven't seen *Pulp Fiction*?' (Participant 7 – FG2).

Evidence from the focus groups reveals participants are very aware of the hype and cultural significance of the target films in their immediate society. The target films are discussed, praised, and vilified by the media and peers alike, and although participants did not claim they chose to see the target films because they were violent, evidence indicates the heightened awareness of participants to the controversy surrounding the target films and their representations of violence is a contributing factor in their decision to see the films. Such an awareness is also significant to the reactive mechanisms of thresholds and self-censorship, with some participants eschewing certain target films because of the violent content, and others deliberately testing their response to infamous representations of violence.

Hollywood versus 'new brutalism'

Participants clearly differentiate between Hollywood action movies, such as the *Die Hard* series, or *Terminator 2*, and the target films. All participants agree dialogue is significant to the target films and their appreciation of them. Evidence of sharp, incisive and intelligent dialogue in such films as *Pulp Fiction* is one of the most significant differences between the target films and Hollywood action movies. In particular, Tarantino is praised for witty, intelligent dialogue and characterization in his films. One participant explains:

> Hollywood action movies are too cartoony at the moment. Something like the *Terminator*, it's just straightforward kind of kids' comic adventure. There is no sophistication in the text, in the dialogue. There's no irony. (Participant 1 – FG4)

Hollywood action films are considered good fun, but the target films possess more thought provoking representations of violence. The target films are more disturbing and challenging because they are more realistic in their depiction of violence. A number of illustrations will serve to highlight this:

> I went to see *Die Hard with a Vengeance* at the cinema. It was very, very violent but it was so funny, so stupid that it made me laugh. It didn't trigger the same as either *Reservoir Dogs* or *True Romance*. They scared me far more. (Participant 2 – FG3)

> In a lot of Hollywood action films thirty people fall over and that's it, it means nothing: it's violence without consequences. (Participant 1–FG3)

> *Die Hard with a Vengeance* or *Terminator 2* are very mainstream Hollywood films, whereas these films are more off beat, more on the fringe, so they can get away with saying more. There's nothing that really, really makes you scream inside about those films, whereas *Reservoir Dogs* and *Man Bites Dog* definitely do. (Participant 3 – FG6)

Participants discuss their heightened levels of fear and adrenalin when viewing the target films as opposed to viewing Hollywood action movies. To be scared, or 'scream inside' is a desired response by Participant 3, and other group members imply they know what to expect from Hollywood action movies whereas the target films can take them by surprise. What is more, the target films represent the consequences of violence; their representations of violence are more real and this difference is praised. Two participants discuss this:

> I think Hollywood movies are far more offensive personally because of the way they portray violence. There's a total lack of reality. I mean –

in *Pulp Fiction* compare John Travolta, when he accidentally blows a guy's head off in the car. In *Die Hard* Bruce Willis never gets covered in bits of bone and brain; his clothes fall off so we get to see a bit more of his body, he gets beaten to a pulp and then gets up and scales an elevator shaft or something. (Participant 4 – FG3)

People like Schwarzenegger or Stallone don't even look real. They look fantastical. Whereas in *Henry, Portrait of a Serial Killer*, Henry is someone you could see walking down the street. You don't know. (Participant 1 – FG1)

Thus, realistic representations of violence are subject to praise because they cannot be anticipated, because they are not formulaic, but based on participants' perceptions of real life experiences: it is because of these factors that participants take these films more seriously than their Hollywood counterparts. However, although participants consider the target films as different to other Hollywood action movies of similar content, this does not mean they do not like to watch Hollywood action movies. As one participant says: 'The *Terminator* films are mainstream, but they're still interesting and a lot of fun to play around with' (Participant 4 – FG6).

The two target films which attract the most praise in the discussion groups are *Pulp Fiction* and *Reservoir Dogs*, two films which are considered to be entertaining, intelligent and part of a cultural zeitgeist. The two films least praised by participants in the discussion groups are *Man Bites Dog* and *Henry, Portrait of a Serial Killer*, two films which adopt documentary style realism and are considered not entertaining. The number of films viewed by participants bears witness to this observation: all 36 participants had seen Reservoir Dogs and Pulp Fiction, 12 of which had seen *Reservoir Dogs* more than once, 13 of which had seen *Pulp Fiction* more than once. In contrast, 15 participants had seen *Man Bites Dog* and 14 had seen *Henry, Portrait of a Serial Killer*, and only one participant respectively had seen either film more than once (See Table 3 and 6).

Although all the target films are perceived as different to Hollywood action movies, certain films within this category are perceived as less entertaining. Therefore, when choosing to see the target films most participants prefer less real, and less disturbing violent films despite the fact that they are aware of and praise the realistic and thoughtful representations of violence in the target films. There are different degrees of realism, and participants choose to see those films which may be realistic but do not challenge the boundary between fiction and reality. For further data analysis see Chapter 7, 'The Question of Entertainment'.

Table 6: Repeated Viewing

FILM	Male	Female	Total
Reservoir Dogs	8	4	12
Pulp Fiction	9	4	13
True Romance	4	1	5
Natural Born Killers	3	1	4
Man Bites Dog	0	1	1
Henry, Portrait of…	0	1	1
Bad Lieutenant	1	1	2
Killing Zoe	1	0	1

Conclusion

Societal/cultural agreement about the target films as extreme and brutalising ensures that most participants are drawn to see these films precisely because of this factor: participants chose to see a film such as *Natural Born Killers* because societal/cultural consensus declares it to be unacceptable. There is a cultural cachet attached to movies such as *Pulp Fiction*, and peer pressure is prominent. However, other factors such as actors, directors and individual preference indicates participants are active consumers, and not wholly influenced by media hype and peer pressure. No participant claimed they chose to see the target films because they were violent; many other social and cultural factors influenced their decision-making processes. One of the most significant considerations is that the target films are different to the usual Hollywood fare, and participants specifically praise the intelligence, humour, dialogue, acting and direction of 'new brutalism' movies. They may enjoy Hollywood action movies, but the target films are more intellectually satisfying, and more demanding of the viewer.

The activity of viewing violence

The process of viewing violence is a conscious activity. Evidence from this study indicates that participants are aware not only of why they choose to see a movie, but also of the specific environment associated with viewing violence. Environment signifies an awareness of context, both in relation to cinema or home viewing and in relation to the context of violent representations themselves. Participants gauge their own response to violence by monitoring audience reaction to violent scenes/images, and they do so whilst at the same time acknowledging the specific context of violence on screen: both activities are comparable.

Audience awareness is closely linked with physical and emotional responses to violent movies. Participants experience a range of physical and emotional responses, such as anger, fear, excitement, disgust: there is no one response to viewing violence. A key factor in the range of response available is the role of anticipation when viewing violence. Anticipation heightens response, increases excitement and emphasizes the significance of preparation: participants anticipate the worst that can happen and prepare themselves for just such an imaginary event. The significance of real experience emerges as central to understanding fictional violence; in this chapter the activity of viewing violence can be seen to be influenced by personal experience, a method of interpretation all participants utilize.

Audience awareness

The majority of participants are aware of audience reaction to violent scenes when at the cinema. Participants mime audience response: placing hands over their eyes, turning away from the screen, squirming in their seats. One participant recalls: 'In *Pulp Fiction* when they do the insulin shot the whole cinema just erupted' (Participant 2 – FG6). Two participants discuss a collective response to *Reservoir Dogs* and the infamous ear-amputation scene:

> We spent the first hour waiting for the ear-slicing scene, then during this scene the entire cinema was saying oh, oh, this is it. (Participant 3 – FG4)

> The cinema was packed, there was definitely an atmosphere, like going to a gig or a play. There was a tangible tension and then people definitely relaxed a lot after the ear scene. (Participant 1 – FG4)

For one participant, one of the reasons he chose to watch *Natural Born Killers* was to monitor his own reaction:

> I think with these films, you go in the cinema and are very aware of other people's reactions, you're expecting it. Especially with *Natural Born Killers*. It was banned, and so you're watching the film partly for yourself and partly to see how others react because it has been hyped up. You want to see how your friends react to all the killings. (Participant 1 – FG1)

Participants were aware that viewing violent movies can be a self-conscious activity and that the nature of a film, and in many cases the media hype surrounding its release, contributes to audience awareness. Most participants recall audience response to infamous scenes from movies such as *Reservoir Dogs*, *Natural Born Killers*, or *Pulp Fiction* precisely because participants are alert to the shared anticipation and excitement specific to viewing such films.

When watching a video in the home environment, participants are aware there is more scope for audience interaction. One participant comments: 'I notice more reactions when I watch videos at home with family or friends. In the cinema there is the big screen and darkness' (Participant 2 – FG1). Another participant comments on the visual effects of violence, specifically blood, and is aware of audience response in the home environment when such scenes occur. She says: 'If there is a lot of blood then I try not to watch it. They [her friends] laugh at me because to me it is quite gory but to other people it's quite funny' (Participant 4 – FG4). This participant self-censors such scenes, and is more conscious of doing so in the home environment than at the cinema. Indeed, her conscious awareness of her specific reaction to scenes involving the visual effect of blood is one of embarrassment (she nervously laughs as she speaks and compares her response to her friends who do not self-censor). Such embarrassment can be traced to the increased visibility of her reactions to a violent movie in the home environment.

This difference in environment highlights the conscious activity of viewing violence, but it also signifies that participants may wish to be part of a more anonymous audience than that available in the home. When at the cinema, participants can monitor their own reactions to violent scenes as part of a larger whole (see Chapter 6, 'Thresholds and Self-censorship', for further discussion).

The significance of context

Context is a key issue when considering the activity of viewing violence. Context is closely linked to environment. Certain films and certain friends do not go together. One participant cites an example of seeing the film *Braveheart* (Mel Gibson, 1995) with a friend who called out and laughed at the violence. Whilst this may have been appropriate to a film such as *Pulp Fiction*, this participant felt embarrassed at his friend's inappropriate response to this movie. He explains:

> I went to see *Braveheart* not long ago with a couple of mates and thoroughly enjoyed it. But, what really annoyed me was that one of my friends sat through all the battle scenes saying: 'oh yes, see his head come off, oh brilliant, oh look at all that blood', and I was thinking

'shut up'. This is not the sort of film where you want to be doing this. You should be saying: 'oh those poor people laying down their lives', not 'oh cool, did you see his arm fly off.' (Participant 3 – FG4)

Another participant comments on the ear-amputation scene in *Reservoir Dogs*:

The TV we watch is so aggressive and Tarantino's films are like that too. The films are TV in the way they move at a fighting pace. People my age don't really dwell on the ear-slicing scene, but when older people see that they think it was a graphic scene, and then they walk out and ask the reaction of kids and they say: 'Great, I loved it'. (Participant 3 – FG1)

For this participant, an older generation is not equipped to respond to the movie in the same way his peers are: they have not been taught what to expect, or told how to anticipate the 'fighting pace' of this film: an older generation does not understand the cultural context of the movie. Whilst this comment is not validated by other group members, it highlights a notion of individuality and distinctiveness concerning this participant's own 'generation' and a desire to retain the cult (i.e. youth) status of Tarantino's movies.

Laughter is a common response participants notice and question. Certain movies generate acceptable laughter, such as *Pulp Fiction*, whilst others, such as *Henry, Portrait of a Serial Killer* do not, and to laugh at inappropriate places risks censure from other members of the audience (see Participant 3 – FG4, earlier in this discussion). Participants discuss how sensitive they become to unwanted noise and inappropriate laughter:

I get hyper-sensitive when I'm watching a film and I can hear the slightest noise anywhere – it drives me absolutely mad. The worst film I ever saw was *The Texas Chain Saw Massacre* (Tobe Hooper, 1974). Everybody in the audience just seemed to be laughing constantly, as loud as possible, just to impress their mates; to say: 'I'm not affected by this, it doesn't upset me at all'. I wished they'd just shut up and watch the film. (Participant 4 – FG6)

Another participant recalls seeing *Braveheart* and laughing at a violent image which he did not find comical:

A guy falls to his death and everybody laughed at that and I felt as if maybe I should laugh with them, and I did. I can't understand why I did that. I suppose you try to fit in with everybody else so you're not left out. (Participant 3 – FG6)

The one scene participants frequently cite as an example of laughter and the conscious activity of viewing violence is the Marvin scene in *Pulp Fiction*. One participant comments:

When Marvin gets his head blown all across the back of the car, I thought that was really funny, but it seemed the audience were divided. Half burst into laughter and another half thought it was absolutely shocking. (Participant 3 – FG4).

Humour can relieve tension, but it can also divide response, those who do not laugh questioning those who do find violence funny. Context is a key consideration; as one participant says: 'That kind of response is alright in *Pulp Fiction*, but if everybody starts going "ah, please" in the middle of *Man Bites Dog* you'd go mental' (Participant 4 – FG6).

In all the examples cited, no participant compared an awareness of laughter and screen violence with laughter and other movie genres. This laughter is accompanied by a visually violent scene, and is recognized as different.

Participants place specific emphasis on the correct way to respond to certain violent films; sensitivity to the context of violence is significant, and an awareness of those moviegoers who do understand this significance places all the more emphasis on the moviegoer who knows how to respond appropriately to specific scenes. In the case of laughter and the context of violence, participants cite their annoyance and disgust at inappropriate laughter because it signifies the fine line between legitimate and unacceptable response to fictional violence. Aware of societal/cultural consensus of consumers of violent films, participants become hypersensitive to how they should respond, and show an ability to monitor other responses and censure that which is inappropriate to the context of representations of violence.

Gender awareness

Participants are aware of a difference between the way men and women react to representations of violence. Men are perceived as having little reaction to violence, whereas women are more voluble and physical in their response to violence. One participant explains:

> I pay a lot of attention to the way other people react in the cinema. I think there is a difference between the way men and women react to violence and I think a lot of it is a conditioned response. It's okay for women to scream but a lot of men don't feel comfortable doing that kind of thing. (Participant 4 – FG3)

Two female participants recall seeing *Braveheart* and being aware not only of their own response but of other cinema goers' reactions, particularly men. One comments:

> I really loved *Braveheart*; it was very violent, very gory, but I really enjoyed it – we were hiding under our coats – it was very gory. I noticed other people, especially men sit there and have to watch it. We were like this – 'Oh my god that's disgusting' – they were like (mimics serious expression, pursed lips). I was looking around at people and they were half-watching me. (Participant 2 – FG3)

This conscious awareness of other moviegoers and the issue of gender becomes a subject groups debate at length. For example, in one all-male group, one participant said he knew of a female friend whose response was noticeable because it was extreme, and other group members laugh at this comment, also citing examples of other women they know who have similar responses when viewing violence. One participant claims if he goes to the cinema with male friends he is aware that their reaction is a positive reaction, i.e. 'that's cool', whereas if he goes to the cinema with his girlfriend, or in mixed gender company, he is aware that female reactions are different: 'Girls don't like it when someone gets shot'(Participant 3 – FG1).

Some male participants claim they do not notice audience response to violent scenes, however on closer inspection these admissions reveal how aware male participants really are of the shared activity of viewing violence. For example, two male participants comment:

> If I'm watching a film, I don't notice what other people are doing. The only time I do notice is when I feel something like a jump, you know, you feel everyone else doing the same thing. But other than that I don't actually look at what other people are doing. I get the impression they're not doing anything except watching the film. (Participant 3 – FG3)

> I don't think I recognize anyone's reactions in the cinema...I think everyone's sort of socially prepared for these type of films. Obviously when you come out of the cinema everybody starts talking about the film, you all have to shout all at once until you get to the pub. But I don't think I've ever heard anyone scream or stand up in the cinema and go: 'ah no, look, they've just cut his ear off' and run out. (Participant 2 – FG4)

In each example, the participants concentrate on their own non-responsive state when viewing violence: for one participant, watching the movie is the main priority of the audience, for the other, preparation is the key. Both speak as an individual member of the audience, and for the audience as a whole. Both participants claim to not notice audience response, yet show just such an awareness; for the first participant, as soon as he claims not to notice other moviegoers, he mentions audience fear and shock; similarly, when the second participant states his impression that other moviegoers desensitize themselves to violence, this is a tacit admission that he is aware of audience response – he expects their reactions to be similar to his own, i.e. non-responsive.

A further example will illustrate this point. One couple debate the issue of audience awareness and the process of viewing violence. The male partner claims:

> I don't find myself shocked very often by violence in films. I think if you're shocked you might look around for a reinforcement of your feelings. But, I'm not aware of why I should be looking to see other people's reactions if I'm not reacting myself. (Participant 1 – FG3)

Because he is not shocked by violence, this participant does not feel the need to monitor his response in relation to other moviegoers. In contrast, his partner verbally and physically responds to violence on screen. She replies to his comment:

> If I see something which is shocking then I'll yell out or laugh. It's the shock that makes me laugh. I'll bring my knees up or I'll hide under a coat and then I'll look around to see if anyone is looking at me or other people are doing the same. (Participant 5 – FG3)

His partner's comment of her reaction to violent scenes suggests this male participant is aware of the person sitting next to him when watching the target films, if only from the perspective that his reaction is the opposite to his partner's response. This participant claims he focuses on the movie alone – yet when engaged in conversation with his partner about this subject, he reveals an acute awareness of her reaction to violent scenes and his own non-responsive viewing process. Indeed this may suggest that this participant models his own behaviour on what he perceives as opposite to his partner's reaction to violence in the target films: by reacting in an opposite way to his female partner this participant highlights his own male behaviour.

Such denial of any awareness of audience response when viewing violence is intrinsic to male participants and is further examined in relation to the issue of gender and thresholds and self-censorship in Chapter 6. However, bearing in mind evidence in Chapter 3, 'Consumer Choice and Violent Movies', the issue of gender may appear clearly defined, but on further inspection proves complex and variable. Such is the case when physical and emotional responses are examined in the next section. Here, participants reveal very different responses to those charted above.

Physical and emotional responses

Participants commented on a range of physical and emotional responses to viewing fictional violence. For example, participants note their heart beats faster; they feel hot and cold; tense; nauseous; angry; satisfied; fearful; excited. Group members may flinch; curl up in their seats; close their eyes; half cover their eyes with their hands; cover their mouths with their hands or bury their head in a coat. Such comments were substantiated when participants viewed specific scenes in the discussion. For example, when participants saw a scene from *Henry, Portrait of a Serial Killer* they exhibited distinctive bodily reactions: participants touched their eyes, ears, covered their mouths, steeled themselves and showed tense facial muscles. Not only did participants exhibit such response during screenings, the memory of certain violent images was so strong many participants re-enacted their physical reponse during the discussion. One group member even claimed she felt a specific sense of smell, a smell that made her put her hand to her mouth as she described it in the discussion.

A number of examples will help to illustrate the variety of response when viewing violence. One participant describes a sense of excitement when watching violent movies, an excitement she believes to be linked to feelings of anger:

> I get palpitations; it's quite awful to admit but I often feel a sense of excitement when I watch violence. If I'm totally truthful it's suppressed anger working its way out. When I go to see a violent film I often feel quite high after I've seen it…The films can breed excitement. (Participant 4 – FG3)

Another participant discusses feeling nauseous:

> If I see something really violent I start to feel ill, my stomach feels like its going to be sick. If it is really gory and horrible then I'll feel quite dizzy. When you get that horrible dread-like feeling and your stomach just sinks, that's what I feel. (Participant 2 – FG3)

One participant recalls watching *Man Bites Dog* and due to the film's hard-hitting and realistic depiction of violence felt tense and ill at the end of the film. He explains:

> You do tense up. During the film you're not actually releasing any of this adrenalin or tension, you're just sitting there, and after a while you almost feel like you're going to burst. After seeing a film like *Man Bites Dog* I wanted a stiff drink. There were some really horrific bits in it. I don't think it's a very healthy thing feeling that way. (Participant 3 – FG6)

Another participant describes a sense of anticipation and dread when watching *Henry, Portrait of a Serial Killer.*

> I can just feel a prickly sensation on my neck, feel the colour just draining out of you. I mean it's just awful. There is a slow, really obvious build-up to the film – you know what's going to happen, you just know you can't stop it. It's kind of fascinating. (Participant 4 – FG6)

What participants describe here, are a range of physical and emotional responses which are very powerful and memorable. Certain scenes from specific films produce intense response, and part of the process of viewing violence is to anticipate and explore such feelings. From the range of examples cited here it is possible to see participants gain different levels of enjoyment from experiencing intense physical and/or emotional responses. Evidence suggests participants may expect, even desire, to be shocked or excited, to feel a rush of emotions when viewing fictional violence.

Although both male and female participants discussed response to viewing violence equally, there were one or two noticeable differences in methods of response. For example, many female participants use their hands to cover their eyes, mouth, or ears when watching a violent scene. Whilst some men discussed and exhibited similar signs during the focus groups, there were far fewer male participants who responded in a similar fashion: protecting the face with hands appeared to be more specific to female participants. Another difference to emerge from the focus groups was the way in which female participants often responded in a more emotive way to images of violence than male participants. At first this appeared to be a stark difference in response, but as the groups progressed, more male participants revealed emotive responses to fictional violence and appeared to share what had at first appeared to be a specifically female trait in the discussions.

This observation is included here to highlight the way in which male and female participants over a period of time exhibited similar physical and emotional responses. Unlike other sections in this data analysis (such as 'Gender Awareness' in this chapter) where gender difference is noticeable, here it is not a significant factor. What this may suggest is that whilst other areas of discussion highlight gender difference, the immediacy of discussing physical and/or emotional response to viewing violence proves to be an area which male and female participants feel confident and uninhibited in discussing. Therefore, it is significant that when discussing what participants actually feel whilst watching a violent movie, there is no marked gender division, a factor which aids later discussion regarding the apparent difference and then increasing parallels with male and female response to viewing violence.

The role of anticipation

Evidence from the focus groups reveals that anticipation has a key role to play in physical and/or emotional response to fictional violence. Group members emphasize the importance of anticipation when experiencing physical emotions, and they claim this can be part of the enjoyment of viewing the target films. When at the cinema, participants recall placing their hands over their eyes, turning away from the screen, and gripping their companion's arm to both alleviate and heighten their sense of excitement and fear. When at home, participants recall running out of a room when they anticipate certain violent scenes in a film and such an experience is both exciting and frightening, and is specific to home viewing.

When anticipating violence, participants imagine possible outcomes of events, attempting to guess how far the director will go in utilizing the visual effects of violence. One participant explains: 'I anticipate something violent is going to happen all the time. The worst, you know, like they're going to decapitate someone and eat their brains' (Participant 2 – FG4). Many participants imagine the worst possible outcome for a violent scene, playing a game with individual expectation and the director's imagination.

Media hype and friends' response can influence anticipation, and many participants claim they had heard about the violence in certain target films before seeing them – *Reservoir Dogs* and the ear-amputation scene being one example (See Chapter 8). However, this does not necessarily lead to an attenuation of response. Certainly, comments detailed in this chapter would indicate knowing the outcome of an infamous scene can add to the excitement and range of emotions participants experience when viewing violence. Although this is not the case for all participants, many spoke of the build-up of tension and anticipation in the audience when viewing *Reservoir Dogs* or *Pulp Fiction* and this was seen as part of the excitement of viewing such movies. Prior knowledge of a violent film can engender shared anticipation which in turn heightens physical and emotional response.

There was praise for the target films and their specific representations of violence. One group member says:

> With a major Hollywood film you know the violence is coming because of things like music and scene building – you definitely know what's going to happen in a *Terminator 2* situation but with the new sort of violent cinema I think its more difficult to anticipate the violence and that makes it more challenging. It is much more interesting and imaginative. (Participant 4 – FG3)

Many participants echoed this comment, declaring they enjoyed the challenge of anticipating a violent scene when the movie itself left little clues as to how the scene would develop. Such comments suggest that for these participants the challenge of anticipation heightens critical response, a factor which will be of interest to further research regarding the significance of critical response to violent movies.

The process of anticipating fictional violence is also dependent on context and types of movies. Participants profess most of the time that they can anticipate the violence in a film; however certain contexts, such as the Marvin scene in *Pulp Fiction*, do not allow for anticipation – and when this occurs, physical emotions are heightened, in some instances retrospectively. Participants claim certain types of violence can be anticipated, for example a scene involving torture, but others cannot, for example, a scene involving random violence. Participants cite the Marvin scene in *Pulp Fiction* as an example of random violence, and the ear-amputation scene in *Reservoir Dogs* as an example of torture (see earlier passages in this chapter and Chapter 8, '*Reservoir Dogs*: a Case Study').

Discussion of specific scenes reveals the way in which participants fuse anticipation and emotional response with close attention to the aesthetic constructs in a film. The male homosexual rape scene in *Pulp Fiction* produced a number of responses:

> In *Pulp Fiction* there's the bit where Marcellus and Bruce Willis are taken by these people and put into a pawn shop, and you feel Oh shit, they're going to be tortured to death and you're tensing up and you're feeling what's happening in this room is going to be terrible. And then Marcellus is taken away and you hear this squealing voice and you feel he's being killed. This is like hell, I can't stand to look, and when you realize what's really happening you laugh to release the tension because what you were expecting hasn't actually happened. (Participant 3 – FG6)

> Basically we're boys together and the two characters are unwilling participants and that scene gets you to sit back and think, fuck this. It's a relief that they actually get out of it and you think ah ha, your come-uppance. (Participant 1 – FG6)

> I think it's just a case of what's implied is worse than what happens. The scene gets your mind going and then pulls back and you think, god, thank goodness for that. (Participant 2 – FG6)

In this scene two heterosexual men are captured and one is raped by two sadomasochists in a pawn shop. Here, the rape scene is discussed as unpleasant and hell-like; participants note their increasing sense of anticipation and dread as the scene reveals the extent of what both heterosexual characters can expect: rape and torture. When Butch (Bruce Willis) escapes during the rape of Marcellus (Ving Rhames) it is a matter of honour that he kill his potential torturers and save Marcellus any further degradation. Anticipation and expectation are heightened when it is none other than Bruce Willis, well known for his action roles, who retaliates with force and such action creates a sense of satisfaction and excitement for these participants. The fact that these participants have prepared themselves for an act of violence far worse than is shown only increases their sense of anticipation and adrenalin.

Not only do participants refer to types of movies or notorious scenes when considering anticipation and context, sequences within scenes and choice of weapons are perceived as equally important. One participant describes his various physical/emotional responses to different scenes in *Reservoir Dogs*:

> With some scenes in *Reservoir Dogs* I actually felt particularly sick. One of the bits that affected me much worse than the ear bit was when Mr Blonde doused the cop in petrol, and I just thought this is really sick; I could imagine being in that position. Whereas some of

the other scenes were so over the top they were laughable. (Participant 1 – FG4)

Another participant describes how his physical and emotional response to a scene involving Alabama (Patricia Arquette) and a hit man in *True Romance* fluctuated according to his own levels of anticipation and expectation. He says:

> The bit where Alabama is getting beaten up by the hit man I find particularly disturbing, but then again, when she turns the tables on him, whacking and shooting him, I do find that exciting: 'yeah, this piece of scum, give it to him.' It's complex: different sorts of violence for different occasions. (Participant 3 – FG4)

Another participant explains her reaction to the use of knives in individual scenes:

> If it is a knife scene, it really makes me feel very confused and upset. If it is a gun, then I feel very different. It is the context of the violence – (with a knife scene) I kind of freeze and it gives me an all over feeling of great distress. (Participant 5 – FG3)

Other group members agree; their physical emotions are heightened when knives, or familiar, household weapons are used to torture someone and this is because participants can relate to a knife as a weapon, and can also relate to the pain such a weapon inflicts, whereas participants consider guns to be unfamiliar and depersonalizing when used in the target films, and this is because guns are so rarely seen in the United Kingdom. Two participants explain:

> I don't like one-on-one violence when it looks like it really hurts, and they use knives. Shooting's not the problem – it's torture or instant pain. (Participant 2 – FG3)

> Guns are something that no one here has any experience of, I certainly don't, but knives – everybody's cut themselves. The idea of being attacked by a knife is something everyone can visualize. (Participant 1 – FG3)

What such comments reveal is that participants consider individual scenes, sequences within scenes and choice of weapons in relation to real life experience. This has implications for methods of response to violent movies, for participants' physical and emotional reactions to viewing violence are dependent on context and reference to individual experience. Response to fictional violence is collateral with a personal understanding of violence in real life, and although participants may not directly relate to acts of fictional violence, they bring personal knowledge, such as cutting oneself with a knife, to their interpretation of violent acts. In the next section it can be seen that participants approach characterization in a similar way, utilizing context, anticipation, and personal experience as a means of engaging with specific characters in a violent scene.

Conclusion

Viewing violence is a social activity. Participants are aware of other moviegoers' response to fictional violence and monitor their own response according to others. Physical and emotional response to fictional violence is complex and fluid and dependent on context and individual choice. Participants anticipate and prepare for representations of violence, and through doing so activate methods of choice in relation to individual response. Anticipation, context and individual experience shape the process of viewing violence and generate active and dynamic moviegoers.

5
Building character relationships

Participants were shown the eye-stabbing scene from the film *Henry, Portrait of a Serial Killer* (John McNaughton, 1990, prod. 1986) and asked if they could identify with any one character in this scene. Response to this question indicates participants do not identify with any one character, but build character relationships. These relationships are dynamic and fluid. There is evidence participants utilize a number of factors in building character relationships: consumer choice, personal experience and preferences, imaginative hypothesizing and character expansion. These factors combine to create complex and varied interpretations of this scene. It is how participants respond to specific characters, rather than who they identify with, that is most significant to this study and the process of viewing violence. Before examining participants' response, a brief summary of the eye-stabbing scene will be provided.

Summary of scene

Context
The context of this scene is as follows: Henry (Michael Rooker) is a serial killer who, although holding down a job as a pest control man, commits acts of murder as if human beings are no more than vermin who need to be exterminated. He shares a flat with Otis (Tom Towles), an ex-con, and when Becky (Tracy Arnold), Otis' sister comes to stay, Henry develops his relationship with both members of the family. He teaches Otis how to kill, and strikes up a 'romance' with Becky. However, events take a turn for the worse. This is where the eye-stabbing scene occurs, and it signifies the end of Henry's relationship with Otis (in this scene) and Becky (at the end of the film).

The eye-stabbing scene
Henry (Michael Rooker), the central character, is walking in an urban area. It is night time and he walks past two neon signs which say: 'Rose Pest Control, Rose Exterminator.' The scene cuts to the floor of an interior room where a man, Otis (Tom Towles), is raping his sister, Becky (Tracy Arnold). Both are in a state of undress, and Becky is crying out in pain. Henry climbs the stairs to an apartment building. We see Becky struggling to get away from Otis; she is lying face down and attempting to crawl away from her brother, crying 'No'. She does not succeed in escaping and Otis commits anal rape and at the same

Figure 1: Henry, Portrait of a Serial Killer: 'Becky and Henry'

in the discussion claims she felt sick after the screening – yet her main comment concerning the scene is that she could not identify with any one character because the acting and direction were so bad:

> I found the rape scene really disgusting and horrible. That was the only bit that disturbed me in the whole scene, that horrible bit, the rest of it I found ludicrous. It was just ridiculously acted. The bit where Henry stabs Otis in the heart, I just started laughing. (Participant 2 – FG3)

Despite the fact that this participant finds the rape scene so disturbing she feels physically sick afterwards, her body language and criticism of the acting in the scene counteracts this intense emotional response. Shown out of context and without any biographical information about the characters, this participant's response to this scene is one of fear and derision. Other participants, who also viewed the scene for the first time, reacted in a similar fashion; a critical distancing took place when there was not sufficient context or characterization to sustain emotional response, yet this critical distancing in many ways disguised the shock of seeing screen violence as arbitrary and without motivation.

A common misreading for those who have not seen the film before, and are not given information about the scene before screening, is that Otis and Becky are engaged in violent sex at the start of this scene. Two participants explain their response:

> I thought they were having a funny sex game, and that was her boyfriend. When Henry came and kicked Otis off her, I thought she stabbed the bloke who was saving her through the eye. I got completely confused. (Participant 2 – FG3)

> Initially I wasn't sure whether it was a rape scene or whether they were just having violent sex. And then after the first few seconds I thought, no, he is raping her because he is strangling her, and then I did start to feel some kind of unease, I started feeling more tense and disgusted by the scene. (Participant 4 – FG3)

In discussion, participants argue that out of context and with no previous knowledge of the characters, Becky and Otis' actions are ambiguous until Henry enters the room. Rather than first assuming Otis is raping Becky, these participants consider Becky and Otis are engaged in violent sex. Here, lack of context can be linked to a lack of anticipation or preparation for the violence in this scene. A subtle form of self-censorship takes place amongst some participants which is of interest when considering the social threshold of rape and methods of self-censorship in Chapter 6.

After participants (viewing this scene for the first time, without any biographical information) had discussed their response to the characters, information regarding the relationship between Otis, Becky and Henry was given, and a second response monitored. Some participants re-appraised their reaction to the scene; the rape scene now appeared more disturbing and the treatment of Otis more justified: Henry's actions were understandable under such extreme circumstances. However, for other participants this information had no effect on their initial response to the scene. Reasons for not identifying or engaging with this scene were cited by participants as lack of context, yet when given contextual information some participants did not alter their response to the scene. One reason could be that when initially asked to watch the scene these participants felt both disorientated and disturbed by the content matter; asked to make a judgement which they would not normally make under such restricted circumstances, participants felt hesitant to re-appraise this response once it had been made.

Other participants who were shown this scene, and given information about the characters before the screening (but have not seen the film before), reveal their responses to be more confident in relation to participants who were not given character information (and also have not seen the film before) – although, it should be noted both sets of responses were just as open to variation. Similarly, participants who have seen the entire film before exhibit more confidence in discussing characterization, but such response to the characters is still varied. This suggests that whilst context is very significant to the identification process, it is important when and how this context is applied.

Participants who know the film are prepared for the extreme violence in this scene and understand the motivation behind such violent acts. Such awareness of context and biographical information creates confidence in responding to the characters in this scene. The less information and preparation available, the less likely participants are to be confident in forming judgements about their response to Becky, Otis and Henry; there is a scale of response which is comparable with a scale of understanding.

Context and biographical information are important to characterization, but a lack of such information does not necessarily block or attenuate all response to characters seen out of context. In the next section it can be shown participants aid context and characterization by utilizing their own imagination and personal experience. These two factors affect the scale of response by increasing understanding about certain characters, characters which participants wish to know more about.

Therefore, although restrictions placed by the moderator, and by the film itself, on information regarding character motivation may distance some participants, it also generates a desire to augment what character information there is in order to aid contextualisation.

Personal experience and imagination

The ways in which participants respond to the three characters in the eye-stabbing scene from *Henry, Portrait of a Serial Killer* are influenced by individual choice as much as context and characterization. Participants reflect on their own personal experience, preferences, and imagination in order to choose which characters they wish to build a relationship with. For example, some participants may relate to one character because they prefer this character's way of dealing with events, yet they may also engage with another character in the same scene because they understand this character's emotions. The question is not whether participants can identify with any one character, but how they choose to engage with different characters, sometimes seperately, sometimes simultaneously, in the same scene.

Such individual choice is in turn influenced by how realistic characters appear in the light of participants' personal experience. Participants most often begin by stating: 'If I were in the same situation...' before offering response to Henry, or Becky, and such a preface signals how participants merge fictional scenarios with hypothetically real situations. Response to the characters of Henry, Otis and Becky will serve to illustrate this.

The character of Henry

Henry is the most popular character participants claim they can engage with in the eye-stabbing scene. One participant explains his response:

> I don't know if the right word is sympathize or associate with Henry. He does seem to be the gentleman killer chap. He is actually being very gentlemanly and diplomatic about going out with Becky, he doesn't actually sleep with her when he gets the opportunity. So, when Otis, her brother, is sort of raping her, yeah, I think I'd be in exactly the same circumstances: come back to the flat – 'what the hell are you doing?'- beat the shit out of him. So, I think I would associate with Henry. (Participant 2 – FG4)

Another participant compares his own life to that of Henry:

> I identify with Henry because I see an amazingly violent film, and I want be in that situation for an hour and a half, and then I get out of the cinema and it's all out of the window. My personal life is non-violent. That's why I identify with Henry: me and Henry both need our dose of violence but we don't need to bring it home. (Participant 3 – FG1)

In each example, both participants consider their own personal experience: they pose the question 'how would I respond to this situation?', and answer it by fusing an understanding of the fictional world depicted in the film, and the real world the participants inhabit. For the first participant this manifests itself as a close examination of Henry's reasons for killing Otis; he may be a serial killer, but in this instance his actions are justified; he is a 'gentleman killer' drawn to extreme violence because his girlfriend's brother has raped her and Henry is in a position to exact revenge. Although this participant does not say he wishes to be Henry, he understands the need to exact revenge for a violent act towards a loved one. Such understanding, based on this participant's own personal experience and preferences, activates an engagement with the character of Henry. What is more, this participant imagines feelings and motives the character of Henry does not possess in the film. Henry is not a 'gentleman killer', yet it is important for this participant to perceive him as such in order to build a relationship with Henry; if Henry was not a gentleman killer then his actions in this scene would not be justified and this participant would not be able to relate his own hypothetical re-telling of the scene to the fictional scenario. The second participant uses the concept of a fictional film to explain why he understands Henry's anger at violence in his own home: this participant would also not wish to bring violence home: it is there to be experienced in the cinema. Once again, an imaginative re-working of the character of Henry into a serial killer who values the safety of his own home enables this participant to hypothesize that character and viewer have something in common.

When participants claim they can relate to Henry's actions they do so because Henry's actions are instinctive and understandable given the context of this scene. Many participants draw on their knowledge of the film to understand this specific instance of violence, and it is in such cases that the confidence referred to earlier in this chapter ('Context and Characterization') emerges, a confidence which grows with a detailed understanding of the character of Henry.

One participant explains the way in which he builds a relationship with the character of Henry through anticipating and preparing for his violent actions:

> I'd never seen *Henry, Portrait of a Serial Killer* before, but perhaps I got into the mind of Henry because I knew he was going to kill the two prostitutes. Everyone was saying, 'oh yeah, I wonder what he's going to do now'. He's got his favourite woman in a motel and I said, 'oh right he's going to kill her', and he did kill her. It didn't come as a surprise or shock. Initially Henry didn't inflict any damage to females, he was very courteous, he was a gentleman killer. Actually, the only time I was upset was when Henry went into a shop and I thought he was going to kill the shop owner because he was quite abrupt to him, but

he didn't kill him. (Participant 2 – FG4)

This participant goes on to relate his anticipation of Henry's actions with his own knowledge of violence in the real world:

> I'm sorry to say nine times out of ten I side with the killers. Sometimes you do feel like going mad, and you think, yeah, I wish I could be like them. You want to scream out. If you've ever been to the supermarket checkout and something goes wrong, and you're in a queue and you think, oh let me out of here. I think it's just a cry for freedom. It's a product of the society we live in and it's important to have an open mind when watching these films. Who are we to say if they are right or wrong … In *Henry, Portrait of a Serial Killer* you know that his mother was just a downright whore, and I think that's important. He was being brought up in a depraved society. (Participant 2 – FG4)

This specific utilization of fiction and reality draws on context and characterization whilst at the same time highlighting how significant this participant's own personal experience and opinions are in his relationship with the character of Henry. Anticipating Henry's actions, getting into the mind of the killer, relating the character of Henry and his dysfunctional childhood to the horrors of the everyday world, are specific steps towards engaging with Henry. This participant builds on his knowledge of the film, his knowledge of violence in the real world, his own understanding of the frustration Henry feels in order to create ties between the viewer and character, ties which could not be made without drawing on personal experience and the ability to create details, motives and emotions the character does not possess in the film itself. Once again, this participant does not wish to be Henry, but he interprets the character of Henry in a complex and personal way.

The character of Otis
Many participants base their engagement with the character of Henry on their hatred of Otis. One participant comments:

> Taking it completely out of context, assuming I walk in and I know the woman, but I don't know the man, then maybe I would bash them quite severely. I don't know. I think it's hard to judge taken out of context. I think you'd side with Henry. Nobody is going to side with Otis the rapist, and if they do they're sick. (Participant 3 – FG4)

This participant begins by revealing a hesitancy regarding the formulation of an opinion based only on this scene, and not the movie as a whole. However, despite this hesitancy, this participant does have an opinion and reveals he can relate to Henry's actions precisely because he too would react in a similar fashion if in the same situation. This participant believes no one would identify with Otis, and it is possible to see the train of logic that leads him from sympathizing with Henry's actions to acknowledging his abhorrence of the actions of Otis. In many ways, it is because Otis' actions in this scene are so odious, that the character of Henry can appear attractive.

Yet there is evidence that a few participants do feel sympathy for Otis. One participant comments on the feminine screams of Otis as he dies; these are realistic and disturbing and he is affected by this. Another participant says: 'I identified with the rapist at one point because he's holding Henry, he is in pain, he's screaming "I'm gonna die, I'm gonna die" and I sort of felt sorry for the bloke even though he raped his sister' (Participant 5 – FG1).

Although such comments were rare, the fact that they exist reveals participants can briefly sympathize with a character's pain, even if they consider that character abhorrent. Such sympathy does not lead to identification, and does not mean participants cannot vary who they relate to at any given moment in the eye-stabbing scene. Relating to Otis' pain as he dies can be collateral with relating to Henry's anger at discovering Otis had raped Becky. The character of Otis exemplifies the way in which participants can engage negatively with one character and positively with another, while at the same time using personal preference and experience to choose how and when such engagement takes place.

Positive comments regarding Otis were made by male participants, yet this does not mean such sympathy for Otis was exclusive to men, and is as much to do with the lack of comments per se, rather than comments based on a gendered response. Most participants, whether male or female, chose to regard Otis as a means to justify the actions of Henry, not as a character they wished to engage with. As shall be shown with the character of Becky, such refusal to discuss a character is deliberate and serves to highlight individual choice and issues of self-preservation.

The character of Becky

Like Otis, Becky is an example of a character most participants choose not to engage with. Rather than hypothesize what they would do in a similar situation to that of Becky in this scene, participants choose to hypothesize from the character of Henry's point of view. Becky may evince sympathy, but most participants do not wish to build a relationship with her based on personal experience and imaginative expansion of her character. Indeed, in many instances Becky's actions are undermined, and participants hypothesize their own response would be very different to that of Becky in this scene, creating aspects of Becky's character which are not evident in the film or scene in order to validate such reasoning.

Many female participants shut themselves off from discussion about the character of Becky, claiming she is too unreal, or pathetic a figure to relate to. Many male participants believe Becky's violent actions towards Otis are too unbelievable and this creates a barrier to building any form of relationship with her. Although reponse to Becky was not exclusively male vs. female, it was enough to delineate a clear gendered response to the character of Becky which was not visible when considering the character of Henry, or Otis.

Few female participants actually discussed the character of Becky in any great detail. Those that did revealed an ambivalent attitude, and a conscious desire to distance themselves from her situation. Two participants comment:

> I feel if I had to identify with any one of them it would be the woman, but I didn't feel a great deal of sympathy or empathy for her. I'm not sure how much you would identify with her even if you watched forever. (Participant 4 – FG3)

> Becky is poor, white trash with no hope in life. (Participant 1 – FG5)

This distancing technique is an act of self-preservation. Participants ask: 'who would want to be Becky?' Based on the fictional experience of this character, and participants' own personal experience, Becky does not possess the same attraction as Henry, a character who may be violent, but within the context of this scene is justifiably violent. One participant highlights this. She says:

> If I walk into a room with the same two people (Becky and Otis) I will associate with Henry, rather than the girl, and protect the victim. Yes, I would try my best, because I have learnt kung fu in China. I've learnt self-defence. (Participant 4 – FG4)

As with the other participants, she introduces real details from her own life (kung-fu classes) in order to build a relationship with the character of Henry. She would defend herself in a similar situation, therefore she aligns her imaginary actions with those of Henry, not Becky, despite the fact that Becky also perpetrates a violent act. The essential difference is that Becky commits an act of violence after she has been raped by her brother and then quickly returns to the role of victim once more; Henry defends himself and Becky without having to make the transition from victim to aggressor; he is the aggressor exacting revenge, and participants find this far more desirable than Becky's transition from victim to aggressor to victim. When faced with considering: 'would I stab my brother in the eye after he had raped and attempted to murder me?' participants estimate they wouldn't be in that situation in the first place: they would be the protector not the protected.

It is Becky's own act of violence that causes participants to question and/or curtail their response to her character. For most female participants, this act of violence is not acknowledged, although for those female participants who do sympathize with Becky, this action is cited as something they applaud. The majority of male participants believe Becky would not have stabbed Otis in the eye with the sharp end of a metal comb. Two participants discuss this:

> She had no idea how to be incredibly violent and in most situations like that she would want to get up and leave the room. She doesn't care. She doesn't want to be there. And then to go to the other extreme and stab him in the eye is not real. If it was me, the first chance I'd get I'd run and call the police. (Participant 3 – FG1)

> I identify with the lady and her emotions, being raped that way. But everything was smashed when she stabbed him in the eye. I thought it was too extreme. I don't think she would have stabbed him in the eye, perhaps in the back or the stomach, but in the eye was too gruesome. I thought she would have been weak from her attack and just lain there on the floor and let Henry do everything. (Participant 2 – FG1)

In both instances, each male participant considers Becky's violent reaction within the context of their own personal experience and fictional hypotheses. They do not believe Becky to be capable of such an action against her brother; the eye-stabbing is perceived as unreal and therefore unjustifiable; aspects of Becky's character are augmented (for example, her weakness, her practicality) in order to validate these fictional hypotheses. As one participant explains:

> Your initial reaction is to loathe the guy who is raping the girl so much that almost anything becomes acceptable: it's almost an excuse for that level of violence. But when she stabs him in the eye, I thought, was that necessary? (Participant 1 – FG3)

A few participants defend Becky's response:

> I can't really say from a woman's point of view, but if I got raped by a bloke I'd do as much damage as I could. (Participant 5 – FG1)

> It's quite hard to watch something like your eyes being damaged. I think most of us have a fear of our eyes being hurt like that. In the context of Henry I do think you need to see that violence. Participant 3 – FG4)

However, the predominant response to Becky's act of violence is to question and then reject the validity of her stabbing Otis in the eye.

Although the direction and special effects are significant in relation to this criticism, it is also relevant to consider whether participants find it difficult to accept Becky's actions because they are a) gruesome, and/or, b) she is female. No one questions Henry's violent actions later in the scene, despite the fact that in terms of style and choice of weapon they are very similar.

Both the lack of female participants' response to Becky, and the questioning of the eye-stabbing by male participants is of interest to later discussion regarding thresholds and self-censorship, in Chapter 6. The fact that Becky is violently raped (and this anal rape is filmed in a manner that is both real and very disturbing) appears to effect female participants to the extent that the majority refuse to discuss her character at all. The level of realism and the sordid fact that this is incest shuts off most female participants' desire to build a relationship with the character of Becky. When considering the character of Henry, both male and female participants claim they could engage with his act of violence, yet although Becky also exacts her revenge, and her act of violence is defensive, this does not draw the majority of female participants to relate to her actions. Further textual and theoretical analysis will be useful in examining why the character of Becky is so difficult to relate to, and why the social taboos of incest and rape overshadow the defensive reactions of Becky, a reaction which becomes problematic for many male participants precisely because she stabs Otis in the eye. Certainly, in relation to the social threshold of rape, discussed in Chapter 6 'Thresholds and Self-Censorship', the majority of male participants expressed a desire to protect the fictional female rape victim. The fact that both male and female participants relate to Henry's actions is an indication that the majority of participants wish to associate themselves with the protector not the protected.

Conclusion

One participant made this comment with regard to the process of identification:

> When you go into the cinema you should leave your conscience or opinions at the door and pick them up on the way out. For that reason, if you do leave them, you are able to identify and connect with people you wouldn't normally connect with. (Participant 3 – FG1)

However, evidence from the focus groups would suggest the exact reverse is the case. The majority of participants do not claim to 'identify' with any specific character but prefer to use other means of expression to describe the variety of response to the eye-stabbing scene from *Henry, Portrait of Serial Killer*. Participants utilize personal experience and opinions in order to engage with character(s) of their choice. Context, characterization, realism and imagination all play a part in how participants build character relationships and these specific methods can be used as a means to understand fictional violence, allowing participants to select the level and type of engagement they wish to experience.

The manner in which participants utilize personal experience is of particular significance in the next chapter, 'Thresholds and Self-censorship'. Participants anticipate and respond to fictional violence by recognizing the role context and characterization have to play in the viewing process. The fact that participants draw upon personal preference and experience when emotionally responding to the characters and actions in a violent scene only serves to highlight how participants are aware of possible thresholds; the process of identifying a threshold is very much part of anticipating and preparing for a type, or level of violence participants know they personally find disturbing.

6

Thresholds and self-censorship

The reactive mechanisms of thresholds and self-censorship prove to be central to the process of viewing violence. 'Thresholds' signify different types and contexts of violence which participants find personally disturbing. 'Self-censorship' signifies methods of choice in relation to watching/not watching violent movies. Both areas are fluid and dependent on context, and both areas denote complexities of response to fictional violence.

Examples of types and contexts of violence participants find disturbing reveal there are social and personal thresholds to viewing violence. Social thresholds indicate participants identify a type of violence they find personally disturbing, but this violence is a common fear shared by a number of other participants; the process of identifying this threshold is collective rather than subjective. Personal thresholds indicate participants identify a type of violence they find personally disturbing, but unlike social thresholds, reasons for this can be traced to a subjective experience unique to that individual.

Participants use a number of different methods with which to self-censor, ranging from self-censoring types of movies, for example horror, to types of images, for example knives. Self-censorship involves physical barriers, where participants use their body to withdraw from viewing violence, and mental barriers, where participants choose to concentrate on anything other than violent depictions on screen. There are also methods of not self-censoring, where participants prepare for violent representations they wish to watch uninterrupted. The two factors most significant to self-censorship are preparation and anticipation, and these factors enable participants to take an active role in the process of viewing violence.

The issue of gender is noticeable in participants' response to thresholds and self-censorship. The difference between male and female participants' attitude to, and awareness of, these two reactive mechanisms indicates male participants are less likely to identify a threshold or claim to self-censor than women. Women actively use thresholds and self-censorship as part of the viewing process when watching violent movies, whereas men claim to be unaffected by viewing violence. However, as with other gender differences discussed in earlier chapters, the complex and subtle variations underlying this apparent gender division suggest the difference between male and female response to the issues of thresholds and self-censorship is not as evident as it at first appears.

Both male and female participants utilize similar methods of preparation and anticipation, and draw upon what is perceived as specifically male or female responses to viewing violence. Male and female participants are equally aware of the complex and contradictory nature of viewing violence, and the role thresholds and self-censorship has to play in that process. Methods may vary, but participants share similar goals.

Thresholds and self-censorship demonstrate boundary testing. It is through testing boundaries that thresholds are identified and self-censorship utilized. Participants who choose to not self-censor test boundaries in the same way participants who choose to self-censor recognize thresholds and activate self-censorship at a chosen moment in the viewing process. Anticipation and preparation are part of boundary testing; enabling participants to activate consumer choice. It is through boundary testing that participants experience a sense of achievement and/or liberation and this experience is significant to why participants choose to view violent movies: the subject matter of these movies may be extreme, but through individual agency and consumer choice participants interpret fictional violence on their own terms.

This chapter will outline these emergent themes and analyse participants' response to thresholds and self-censorship in relation to the following criteria: social and personal thresholds; methods of self-censorship; boundary testing. Evidence from the discussion groups will indicate participants offer complex and sophisticated responses to viewing fictional violence. Furthermore, this complexity of response is inherent to the process of viewing violence.

Social/personal thresholds

Male and female response to rape: a social threshold
The most common type of violence participants identify as personally disturbing is violence towards women, in particular rape. For heterosexual male participants, rape is a complex issue, and manifests itself as a desire to protect fictional female characters who are attacked/sexually attacked, a desire which can be traced to social/cultural typecasts of the male as protector and the female as the protected. Rape is also a complex issue for female participants, generating both fear and anger at fictional and real incidents of rape. As with male participants, social/cultural typecasts of women as victims influences female participants' response to the issue of rape.

Many male participants refer to the scene in *True Romance*, where Alabama (Patricia Arquette) is beaten, and in turn beats and kills a gangster. As men, these participants wish to save Alabama. Seeing a woman brutally beaten brings out strong feelings of anger and a practical desire to protect the character. However, this scene also brings out feelings of guilt; Alabama is a beautiful woman, and many male participants are attracted to Alabama, yet at the same time angry that she is treated in such a brutal way in this scene. Such ambivalent feelings provoke complex responses to this scene. Two participants comment:

> In *True Romance*, when Patricia Arquette is getting beaten up, you get to see a bit too much violence. It's really hard to watch because you really like her at that point in the film. You want to help her but you can't. You're helpless. (Participant 1 – FG1)

You fall in love with Alabama. Or at least I did. She's so sweet and nice and caring. You don't want to watch her getting beaten up, and when you're watching the violence you expect another character to beat up the bad guy – not just punch him, but cut him in half. The violence provokes a reaction. (Participant 3 – FG1)

Here, these two male participants comment on their attraction to the character of Alabama, whilst at the same time referring to a strong desire to protect her from other male characters in this fictional setting.

The scene itself provokes such a complex reaction because Alabama is depicted as both sexual and aggressive in this scene; her clothes are torn to reveal her body in a provocative way, yet the violence towards Alabama is extreme and unsettling, and as she herself becomes violent, she is transformed from a stereotypical female victim to an atypical female aggressor. Such comments quoted above reveal some male participants respond to the fictional character of Alabama in such a way that she is perceived as both attractive, and vulnerable, and aggressive; a complex range of impressions that provoke complex responses to this scene.

Violence towards women merges with sexual violence in male participants' discussion of this social threshold, and the same desire to protect the victim can be traced throughout – 'the violence provokes a reaction' (Participant 3 – FG1). Two male participants discuss their response to fictional representations of rape:

In *Man Bites Dog* the rape scene was very simple, in black and white, and for some reason I just kept trying to look away. I almost felt like I wanted to jump in the film and get the woman out. (Participant 3 – FG6)

Rape scenes affect me two ways. I either don't like it because they diminish the effect of a rape by titillating it, but at the same time if it is done horrifically, like I believe it should be, it fucking horrifies me. (Participant 1 – FG6)

Female participants discuss the issue of rape from an emotional and critical perspective, both exhibiting fear and anger, and questioning the validity of filmic representations of rape. One female participant actively chooses not to watch films which contain rape and feels this is not a subject for film makers to portray. Watching rape scenes in films such as *The Accused* (Jonathan Kaplan, 1988) or *Man Bites Dog* has had a lasting effect on this participant. She says: 'I hate the personalization of violence: I watch a film like *Man Bites Dog* and think it's me, and it makes me scared for weeks' (Participant 5 – FG2). She echoes many female group members when she criticizes the common occurrence of rape in movies: 'Let's slot in a rape scene' (Participant 5 – FG2) and fears women and men will become desensitized to violence towards women.

The Accused attracted a number of comments by female participants, comments which highlight female participants' fear of rape in real life and their criticisms of the way in which rape is represented on screen. A number of illustrations will serve to highlight this:

Figure 2: True Romance: 'Alabama'

I watched *The Accused* and I was upset for about two weeks afterwards. It was terrible. I don't like the feeling I get from it. I don't like my personal reaction: 'oh God if I watch the rape it could happen.' I don't want to picture what happens. It puts me in a bad mood and makes me feel annoyed and upset. (Participant 2 – FG3)

The Accused is the only film I can think of that I've not seen on purpose because I knew it was all about rape. I don't want to see Jodie Foster get raped because she's someone I admire. I think she's a strong person. (Participant 4 – FG3)

I don't particularly enjoy watching women being raped, but for me it depends so much on context. I found *The Accused* very, very, very upsetting but one of the reasons I found it upsetting is that we only get to see the rape through the eyes of a man. It's only when the guy stands up in court and says: 'I'm the hero, I'm the saviour' that the rape happens. Something like *Straw Dogs* is very distressing; it's about ownership and territory and that extends to women in the film. I think any threshold I have is based on context. I mean, I'm far more offended by *Pretty Woman* than I am *Straw Dogs*. (Participant 1 – FG5)

The first female participant identifies the social threshold of rape as an act of violence she fears will occur in real life; watching *The Accused* has dramatic repercussions. The second female participant cites this film as the only film she deliberately chose not to see because it contained the threshold of rape; building a relationship with the central character in this film would prove problematic and serve to highlight women as victims, not a role this participant associates with Jodie Foster, who is someone she admires – 'a strong person'. The third female participant contextualizes the issue of rape and criticises specific films – *Straw Dogs* (Sam Peckinpah, 1971), *Pretty Woman* (Gary Marshall, 1990) – for their misogynistic portrayal of women; representations of fictional rape are distressing, but certain contexts are more offensive than others. All three examples indicate how participants identify the social threshold of rape, and choose to self-censor, a reactive measure which will be discussed in more detail later in this chapter.

As the last example indicates, not all participants feel rape should not be represented. Whilst representations of rape are considered disturbing, the validity of screening such representations depends on the context within a film. *Man Bites Dog* and *Henry, Portrait of a Serial Killer* are cited as two films which represent rape in such a way that it is both real and shocking. For some women this is unacceptable, however a few group members argue for the validity of such representations in these films. As one woman says: 'You have to push against boundaries' (Participant 2 – FG2).

Response to sexual violence towards women did not lead to response to fictional representations of male rape in the target films. Neither male or female participants discussed fictional representations of male rape as a social threshold. One male participant, when referring to Marcellus (Vick Rhames) in the male rape scene from *Pulp Fiction*, considers the impact of this rape far less disturbing than representations of female rape. He explains: 'I suppose technically I didn't bleed for him as much as I would for a woman, I think women are more vulnerable' (Participant 1 – FG6). Another female participant comments: 'I thought, thank God it's not a women being raped. Isn't that terrible?' (Participant 2 – FG3).

Such comments serve to highlight how participants anticipate representations of female rape, and anticipate they will be disturbed by such scenes. This anticipation does not occur with regard to representations of male rape and it is the lack of representations of male rape which participants highlight as a reason why they do not experience such anticipation. Two female participants comment:

> Two guys getting raped – we never see that. It's very, very rare you see it. And young men in the audience are going to be embarrassed and uncomfortable and laugh at what is a distressing rape scene. (Participant 1 – FG5)

> It's strange because in *The Accused* I obviously empathized with Jodie Foster, but with the two men in *Pulp Fiction* I didn't empathize with them at all because they were men. I mean it was disturbing and horrible to watch but I didn't have the same feelings as I did when Jodie Foster got raped. It was a different kind of rape, a rape for a reason. (Participant 3 – FG5)

Here, two participants comment on a lack of empathy or engagement with the male characters in *Pulp Fiction* and they trace this lack to the unfamiliarity of male representations of rape. It is because female representations of rape are more common in movies that these participants can engage with events, understand the 'reason' for the rape. The first participant's perception of male members of the audience and their embarrassed response to this scene, corresponds with an absence of response by male participants in the discussion groups to this scene, despite the fact that *Pulp Fiction* is considered to be the most popular movie by participants.

Male rape is not a shared fear because male participants do not express a fear of such a violent attack, and female participants do not express a desire to protect male victims of rape. It is female rape which attracts a collective interest and participants' response to female rape confirms societal/cultural fears of this act of violence. Thus, most male participants wish to act as the protector when viewing female rape scenes and most female participants wish to eschew the subject of rape altogether. This social threshold illustrates and confirms social taboos.

Other social thresholds
Participants identified a number of other social thresholds, which, though not as commonly referred to as violence towards women, constitute fears that could be discussed as a collective experiences. One of these thresholds entails violence involving children and animals. One group member comments: 'I'm really not convinced it's safe to portray violence against children and animals on film' (Participant 2 – FG5). For many participants it is the *thought* of a film which exhibits cruelty to children or animals, rather than specific instances themselves, which defines this threshold. As one participant explains: 'If I knew that there was going to be a kid tortured in a film I wouldn't go and see it in the first place' (Participant 3 – FG1). The implicit question is: would any-

one choose to see such a film if it did exist? For all participants, the answer is negative, and by identifying such an emotive threshold, participants can share in a feeling of social responsibility and group acceptance.

Another social threshold identified by participants is violence involving weapons such as knives, or household implements. As discussion regarding the emotional impact of violence in Chapter 4, 'The Activity of Viewing Violence', indicates, it is precisely because group members have personal experience of such violence, knowing what it is like to hold a knife, or cut oneself, that response to such violent acts is so collective. As one participant comments: 'Violence and guns don't enter into our lives' (Participant 7 -FG2), whereas a weapon such as a knife is part of life (see Chapter 4 for further discussion).

A fear of needles and injections also becomes a collective threshold for participants. One participant comments: 'I can't stand to see a needle going in; you get so close and when the camera focuses in I can't bear it' (Participant 4 – FG6). Many participants cited the adrenalin shot in *Pulp Fiction* as an example of this threshold. As one participant explains:

> When the guy was doing the adrenalin thing you had the option to look away; it took so long for him to give the injection, it made you think what would go wrong, what if the needle broke off in her breast plate, oh my God how horrible that would be. I started to do this (acts out putting her hands in front of her face) just thinking about it. (Participant 1 – FG5)

What these collective thresholds share is the way in which participants identify a level or type of violence they find personally disturbing, yet these thresholds cannot be traced to subjective experiences; they are social taboos, reinforced by the very existence of the social threshold itself. One participant comments:

> It very much depends on the individual. For example, I'm not afraid of dead bodies, but really deep, rumbling voices affect me. I'm more afraid of possession and so *The Exorcist* is my nightmare. It depends on your experience and beliefs and what happened to you as a kid. (Participant 3 – FG6)

In the case of social thresholds, personal experience and beliefs are most significant in relation to the ability to be part of a collective fear which is recognized and validated by other group members. As the next section will reveal, childhood memories and personal experience shape personal thresholds, and it is this experience, rather than a group dynamic, which validates a specific threshold for the individual.

Personal thresholds
Personal thresholds re-affirm the effects of personal experience. The transition from social to personal thresholds reveals that many participants' personal thresholds involve the same types of violence identified as social thresholds in the previous section. An example will illustrate this. One participant reveals:

> I really don't like rape scenes now. I have a friend who described her experience of rape; I had no idea it was so traumatic. I used to love *A Clockwork Orange* but now I'd find it difficult to watch it knowing the realities of rape for women. (Participant 3 – FG1)

The threshold of female rape has been identified as a collective fear by other group members; however, what makes this example different to participants' comments in the previous section is the way in which this participant uses a friend's personal experience to shape his own viewing habits, i.e he finds it difficult to watch *A Clockwork Orange* (Stanley Kubrick, 1971) because it contains graphic depictions of rape. The impact of a specific instance of violence has a vivid and lasting effect on this participant, and this personal experience is a main factor in the identification of this threshold. It is this which makes the threshold individual rather than collective.

Many participants have childhood memories which affect personal thresholds. One participant recalls an incident as a child whereby he saw an image of a throat being cut on TV; the memory is vague, but the impact of seeing this image is such that he will not watch any scene involving this type of violence. He says:

> I don't like to see people having their throats cut. You can always tell when that's coming because someone from behind puts a hand over the victim's mouth. I always look away – that is the one thing I don't like to see. I saw something as a child on TV. I remember being quite young and seeing it after school. I'm sure I saw someone get their throat cut. It's the only thing I know I can't really watch. (Participant 1 – FG3)

Another participant finds the visual effect of blood disturbing. She recalls:

> My mum was a nurse in a Chinese hospital, and I saw a lot of blood. I'm always scared of blood, you know, seeing my mother come home and she had been in an operation and sometimes blood would be on her clothes. It makes me scared to see things like that – seeing blood affects me more than anything else. (Participant 4 – FG4)

This participant does not say what she feared as a child – perhaps her mother was hurt in some way – however the effect of this memory is such that she identifies the visual effect of blood as a personal threshold.

Real life experience affects thresholds and the viewing process. A number of group members experienced real life violence and this influenced participants in different ways. For example, one participant witnessed a knife attack not long before the discussion and she made a decision not to watch any violent movies after this attack. She explains: 'I have got to the point where I do align violence with the real act and it bothers me' (Participant 1 – FG2). Another woman was attacked and threatened with a knife, and she identifies any violence involving knives as her threshold. Here, personal experience leads to self-censorship, yet unlike the first participant she does not class all violence as personally disturbing, only specific types. She explains:

> I was attacked, and any violence involving knives physically repulses me. It really brings up all sorts of very strange emotions that I never

feel at any other time. If there is a knife involved I get quite angry, and it has definitely affected me as a person. I have a lot of violence in me. I kind of will my attack to happen again so that I can act it out. I keep thinking 'I wish I could have fought back', and so if I see a rape scene I think, 'wouldn't it be great if she could just do something violent – do this and fucking do that'. (Participant 5 – FG3)

Although this participant experiences anger and fear when viewing fictional violence involving knives, and this is directly related to personal experience of violence, as a consumer she re-lives her attack through watching violent movies where the female victim fights back. Anger is deliberately channelled into a fictional scene of violence where women are seen as aggressors. This participant identifies a personal threshold related to real experience of violence, but it is through this personal threshold that she continues to watch other types of violence, making the process of viewing violence traumatic in certain instances and cathartic in others.

Another participant witnessed real violence but this experience did not effect her viewing habits to any substantial degree. She explains:

I was on the bus one time when a guy was stabbed. I tried to tell the driver to do something about it but you're on a bus and there's very little you can do. I was shaking and in a state of shock after the attack because I knew I had a responsibility and I couldn't fulfil that responsibility. I mean, I've seen violence against friends in the past. I think you learn to avoid violence. I avoid it at any costs. But I go and see these movies because I know it's fiction. (Participant 3 – FG5)

For this participant, the experience of seeing real violence is traumatic and ensures she avoids potentially violent situations at all costs. However, this experience does not lead to an identification of any specific personal threshold when viewing fictional violence. Violent movies are not real and do not equate with real experience of violence. For a more detailed discussion of participants' response to real violence and their perception of fictional violence see Chapter 7, 'The Question of Entertainment'.

There are two points to be made regarding personal thresholds. First, whilst participants may share similar thresholds to others, i.e. rape, or blood, which could be considered social taboos, personal experience means such thresholds have added significance and re-affirm relationships between personal experience and choices and values made in real life. Second, participants who have experienced/witnessed real violence do not necessarily react in similar ways: some may eschew all violent movies, others self-censor specific types of violence, whilst some participants notice no marked difference in their viewing habits. Clearly, examining personal thresholds produces varied results, and the experience of real violence does not necessarily lead to anti-violence attitudes, although in some instances this is the case.

Self-censoring violence

Methods of self-censorship
Participants choose to self-censor violent movies in four ways:

1   Self-censor all violent movies;
2   Self-censor violent movies which contain thresholds;
3   Self-censor violent scenes which contain thresholds;
4   Self-censor violent images which contain thresholds.

There are a number of methods to self-censorship. For example, some participants half watch the screen, covering their face with their hands, or mentally switch off and stare at a corner of the screen, movie theatre, or home
environment when choosing to self-censor. Whilst other participants may
choose different measures and place their head in their hands, hide under their
coat, hide behind sofas, or offer to make the tea when a key scene occurs.
     Some examples will serve to illustrate this. One participant explains his
active self-censorship of horror movies:

> I can't watch horror films. I can watch realistic violence but people
> with white faces coming in and chewing lumps out of one another,
> they frighten me so I don't watch them. I'm outside the door, watch-
> ing through the crack: 'Is it over yet? Fuck me, I'll make the tea'.
> (Participant 1 – FG6)

Another participant reveals how he responds to images of dead bodies in films:

> I watched *Twin Peaks* the other night on video, and they found this
> body and they were lifting her veil and I couldn't watch. It was a dead
> body, she couldn't feel anything, it was obviously special effects, but I
> just couldn't watch it. (Participant 4 – FG6)

A third participant considers her response to the threshold of violence involving eyes; she would half-watch such scenes if they appeared in a film. She
explains: 'I would definitely want to see the scene, I wouldn't want to not see
it at all; but I would be protecting myself, I guess, by watching it through my
fingers' (Participant 1 – FG5).
     All three examples reveal the variety of methods participants use to self-cen-
sor. The first example self-censors types of movies and physically removes himself from the room when such films are screened in the home environment.
The second example chooses not to watch images of dead bodies, even though
he knows the bodies are not real and are only special effects: self-censoring is
a way of not engaging with dead characters on screen. The third example
chooses to self-censor a specific type of violence, yet she half watches through
her fingers in order to view the scene. Here, curiosity is fuelled by the knowledge that this participant can self-censor, but also remain partially engaged
with the film; covering her own eyes is an act of self-preservation as it is eyes
which are subject to violence on screen, yet eyes also register what is taking
place and they are the means to satisfy the curiosity of the viewer. What these
examples illustrate is the active decision-making which takes place when viewing thresholds of violence: if a type of violence is identified as a threshold by
a participant, then self-censorship is a means to personally control the viewing experience.
     Methods of self-censorship divide into mental and physical barriers,
although both barriers can be activated whilst viewing violence. Mental
barriers signify the methods by which participants choose to concentrate on

something other than the events taking place on screen. Two participants explain:

> When something's too violent for me I switch off- I'll step back and say: 'this is a film, I can step out of it'. (Participant 7 – FG2)

> I was telling myself 'it's not real, it's a film, I'm with my friends and we're having a good time'. (Participant 2 – FG5)

This form of self-censorship focuses on the division between fiction and reality when viewing violence: the violence is not real and therefore through highlighting its fictional status these participants are able to dis-engage with events taking place. Physical barriers signify the methods by which participants use their own body, or immediate environment to hide from a threshold of violence. Two examples will illustrate this:

> I always watch a film to the end, but I have covered my eyes in a film. One film I can't watch is *Outbreak* because to me it is a real threat which affects everybody. I find that disturbing and difficult to watch. (Participant 3 – FG4)

> The first time I watched *Reservoir Dogs* I hid my face and stood up and said, 'no, I don't want to watch that'. I was imagining the cop's face, while I was listening to the music and when I came back into the room he had no ear and his face was slashed. I was relieved he didn't do anything more horrible. The ear scene put me off watching the whole film. (Participant 2 – FG3)

In each instance a physical barrier is created in order to self-censor a threshold to violence. The first participant uses his hands, the second participant uses a variety of physical responses – standing up, hiding her face, running out of the room – in order to self-censor. What the second example also illustrates is the way mental and physical barriers can be combined. This participant mentally and physically dis-engages with the scene; she walks out of the room and also concentrates on events that are not taking place in the film itself, using her imagination to distance herself from the actual violence depicted.

The right environment
Different viewing environments have an effect on participants' attitudes to self-censorship. For example, most participants do not walk out of the cinema, but do switch off videos if they find a violent scene too disturbing. Two participants explain:

> It's much easier to switch off a video. We do that all the time. There's lots of videos I've not watched to the conclusion but there is only one film I've ever walked out of in my life. There is a difference. (Participant 4 – FG3)

> There was something the other day I recorded and I was watching it and it was horrible and I turned it off. Then I thought I'll watch it again a bit later and I turned it on and started watching a bit more of

it but I couldn't watch it and turned it off completely. (Participant 3
– FG5)

Participants self-censor more freely in the home environment than at the
cinema. They feel more able to identify thresholds and choose to self-censor
because the home environment is familiar and time is flexible. As both examples illustrate, participants can return to a film many times in the home environment and self-censor a film in stages, whereas at the cinema this would not
be so easy to undertake. Participants consider the cinematic environment to
offer less diversions, and less opportunities to self-censor; they invest time and
money into a social activity where the wide screen demands attention and the
darkness silence.

Certain films are deliberately chosen to be watched in the home environment because there are more opportunities to self-censor. Therefore, although
participants acknowledge that concentration is attenuated in the home environment, certain participants still choose to view specific violent movies on
video. As one participant explains:

> If you're watching something on video you're more likely to shout
> things out and scream and talk and make stupid comments which I
> would never do in the cinema. And, of course, there is that sort of line
> when you're in your own home and you might not accept certain
> things. (Participant 1 – FG5)

Certain participants utilize self-censorship when the line has been crossed and
they do not wish to 'accept' certain levels, or types of fictional violence in their
own home. Two participants discuss why they choose to watch certain violent
movies at home rather than at the cinema:

> I was prepared to see *Reservoir Dogs* on video rather than at the cine-
> ma because I knew that I could obviously walk out of the room or I
> could feel comfortable averting my eyes, or switching off, pick up a
> magazine if it did have a bad effect on me, if I wasn't happy watching
> it. (Participant 5 – FG3)

> *Pulp Fiction* I saw at the cinema because I knew what was going to be
> in it, and it was quite funny rather than being gory and violent and
> disgusting. But, *Reservoir Dogs* and *True Romance* I wanted to watch
> on video rather than at the cinema so that I could not watch it.
> (Participant 2 – FG3)

Both participants cite specific films which they wish to watch at home because
they can self-censor what is 'gory and violent and disgusting'. Methods of self-
censorship involve physical barriers, such as walking out of the room, or reading a magazine, but they also involve the extreme method of switching off the
screen. Indeed, for one participant the knowledge that she can not watch *True
Romance* or *Reservoir Dogs* (i.e. she can self-censor) is a significant reason in her
choosing to view these films in the home environment. The cinema would not
allow such freedom of self-censorship.

Implicit in participants' comments so far is the impression that the home is
a safe environment. However, other participants perceive the home as oppo-

site to a safe environment, and choose to watch specific violent movies at the cinema because they do not wish certain violent movies to *enter* into the home environment. For example, one participant berated her partner for renting *Man Bites Dog*. She explains:

> It was a Saturday night at ten to nine and I said, shall we watch a video tonight, and he came back with *Man Bites Dog*. I thought: 'it's not a Saturday night film'. I got really angry with him for putting it on, and I just said 'I'm not fucking watching this' and I walked out of the room. It's the only time I've ever done that. (Participant 5 – FG3)

Having heard about the violent content of the movie before hand, this participant became angry with her partner for assuming she would enjoy such a movie at home on Saturday night. The time and day are significant; in her opinion this movie is not an entertaining film – something she anticipated for a Saturday night. What is more, she is sensitive to the fact that the movie is in her home in the first place: her home is not a safe place to watch the movie. Here, she is able to choose a specific method of self-censorship: the home environment is not a safe place to watch this film and the reactive mechanism of self-censorship restores a safe environment by enabling this viewer to reject this violent movie.

Other participants comment on the way in which they wish to separate fiction and reality by viewing certain violent movies at the cinema: it is the home environment which makes certain movies appear real. Two examples will illustrate this:

> Watching a film in the cinema is a very safe place to be because you are surrounded by people all having the same effect, they're all scared: then you go out of the cinema and it's a completely different world. When I'm watching a film in my own home it's a completely different experience – it doesn't feel very safe. If I'm the only one there I can't watch certain films because I will become too frightened to carry on watching. (Participant 6 – FG2)

> I prefer to see something at the cinema; it makes it more formal. To see a film on video – I may find that more disturbing. I like a formal separation between my life and what I choose to go and see. (Participant 2 – FG5)

It is possible to see how these participants, unlike the earlier examples, do not find their home environment safe, and do not wish to use methods of self-censorship to establish a safe environment. A 'formal separation' between the fictional world of the film and the real world of the viewer is of primary importance here. Cinema is a social activity and it is precisely a conscious awareness of the audience, outlined in Chapter 4, 'The Activity of Viewing Violence', which these participants choose to experience: the social activity of a cinematic environment emphasises the fictional nature of violent movies.

Audience viewing figures indicate participants choose to watch the target films at the cinema and at home in roughly equal amounts. Tables 7 and 8 reveal *Reservoir Dogs* and *Pulp Fiction* are the most popular movies to have been seen at the cinema, with 25 and 32 participants having viewed each film

respectively, and *Reservoir Dogs, Pulp Fiction* and *True Romance* the most popular movies to have been viewed at home, with 22, 17 and 19 participants
having seen each film respectively. Figures for cinema viewing are higher than
those for home viewing in the case of *Reservoir Dogs* and *Pulp Fiction*, but *True
Romance* scores higher on home viewing, whilst *Natural Born Killers* has
roughly the same figures (12, 13) in each table, despite the fact that it is not
legally available on video in this country.

The Cinema Advertising Association's Film Profile of *Pulp Fiction* and
Reservoir Dogs for August 1996 (see Table 2, Chapter 2, 'Designing the Study')
estimates the total number of people who claimed to see these films at
4,330,000 and 1,344,000, in comparison with *Killing Zoe* or *Man Bites Dog*
which only attracted 250,000, and 286,000 moviegoers. Table 9 reveals that
the number of video retail units sold of the target films corresponds with the
difference in figures noted for cinema viewing. *Pulp Fiction*, for example, sold
371,394 video retail units in 1995, whilst *Killing Zoe* sold approximately
30,000 in 1996, and *Henry, Portrait of a Serial Killer* only sold just under
7,000 in 1996. What such cross referencing reveals is that participants' preference for *Pulp Fiction* and *Reservoir Dogs* at the cinema and on video is typi-
cal of other moviegoers in the Great Britain.

Table 7: Cinema Viewing Figures

Film	Male	Female	Total
Reservoir Dogs	13	12	25
Pulp Fiction	19	13	32
True Romance	6	8	14
Natural Born Killers	6	6	12
Man Bites Dog	1	2	3
Henry, Portrait of...	1	2	3
Bad Lieutenant	4	3	7
Killing Zoe	1	1	

Table 8: Video Viewing Figures

Film	Male	Female	Total
Reservoir Dogs	16	6	22
Pulp Fiction	12	5	17
True Romance	14	5	19
Natural Born Killers	8	5	13
Man Bites Dog	8	5	13
Henry, Portrait of...	7	5	12
Bad Lieutenant	9	2	11
Killing Zoe	7	1	8

Table 9: Video Retail Unit Figures

Film	Distributer/Release	No. of Units
Reservoir Dogs	Polygram Film Entertainment, Aug. 1996	250,000
Pulp Fiction	Beuno Vista Home Entertainment, Sept. 1995	371,394
Henry, Portrait of...	Electric Pictures, Aug. 1996	6894
Bad Lieutenant	Guild Film Distribution, Aug. 1996	24,718
Killing Zoe	Polygram Film Entertainment, July 1996	30,000

No figures for Man Bites Dog or True Romance

Cross tabulation (Tables 7 and 8) reveals *Man Bites Dog, Henry, Portrait of a Serial Killer, Bad Lieutenant* and *Killing Zoe* score more highly on home viewing, and these are all films participants consider realistic and in many cases not entertaining. In contrast, *Pulp Fiction* is considered the most entertaining, and this is the film most participants have seen at the cinema (see Chapter 7, 'The Question of Entertainment' for further details). This may reflect comments made earlier by participants that certain films are chosen to be watched at home because there is more opportunity for self-censorship. However, it may also reflect the availability of certain films on video rather than at the cinema. *Pulp Fiction* and *Reservoir Dogs* received widespread cinematic release for a long period of time (*Reservoir Dogs* was released in January 1993 and is still showing in selected cinemas), whereas other target films received short cinematic release, and quickly became more widely available on video.

Comments made regarding the home and cinematic environment and methods of self-censorship were made by female participants. No male participant claimed to choose one form of environment over another in relation to the violent content of a film. Table 5 indicates there is no substantial difference between the figures for male and female participants' cinema consumption of the target films. 13 male participants and 12 female participants chose to watch *Reservoir Dogs* at the cinema; 6 male participants and 8 female participants chose to watch *True Romance* at the cinema; and, whilst *Pulp Fiction* reveals some difference in figures, 19 male participants and 13 female participants, all other target films attract similar viewing figures regardless of gender. However, Table 6 indicates there is a substantial difference between the numbers of male and female participants who choose to watch the target films in the home environment. 16 male participants as opposed to 6 female participants chose to watch *Reservoir Dogs* on video; 14 male participants and 5 female participants chose to watch *True Romance* on video: each target film scores substantially less in the column for female video viewing figures.

Taking into account comments made exclusively by female participants regarding the home environment as unsafe, these figures would indicate many female participants actively choose to watch the target films at the cinema because it is a social activity and presents a formal separation between fiction and reality. The fact that home viewing provides more opportunities for self-censorship does not influence the majority of female participants to choose to watch violent movies in the home environment.

This fact is of interest when male and female attitudes to self-censorship are considered in the next section. However, before turning to the significance of boundary testing and formal separations between fiction and reality in relation to male and female response to viewing violence, one other issue emerges in connection with self-censorship and different kinds of environment. Participants comment on the increased opportunity to self-censor when reading violent literature as opposed to viewing fictional violence. A number of comments will serve to illustrate this:

> I read the Irvine Welsh novel *Marabou Stork Nightmares*. It's very disturbing because it involves a rape. Reading the book, you can turn off when you want to, you can put it to one side, that's enough I can't read anymore, but I couldn't watch a film about it, I know that. When you

read a book it can be far more visual but you can stop at any page and put the book down. (Participant 3 – FG5)

I remember reading Roman Polanski's autobiography and getting to the bit where Sharon Tate was killed and thinking I've really got to stop now. With books I think you can say 'enough, enough'. It's good to be able to have that control. Participant 1 – FG5)

I've only ever walked out of the cinema once, and that was because the film was extremely dull and I had better things to do that evening, and I even feel guilty about having done that. I've never turned off a video, but I may have looked away for a few seconds. But I read this one book, *American Psycho*, and it was really – Jesus Christ – I had to put it down for a second to get a grip before I started reading again. It was very different. (Participant 4 – FG6)

What these examples reveal is the way in which participants use another medium, literature, in order to gauge levels of self-censorship when viewing violent movies. In each instance levels of choice and individual agency are increased when participants consider violent literature and the way in which they responded to scenes of violence. Participants claim they can put a book to one side, say 'that's enough, I can't read any more' and have some control as a consumer over the experience of reading violent literature. In the final example, this participant claims he has never self-censored a violent image, the only time he recalls leaving a cinema is because a film is boring, not because it is disturbing; yet, when reading fictional violence this participant actively self-censors.

Why participants feel more able to self-censor when reading violent literature is a subject for further analysis. However, examples of participants' response given here, highlight the significance of environment to self-censorship, and the way in which different attitudes to self-censorship are affected by different media, whether these be cinema, video or literature. In each instance, boundary testing takes place, and in the next section participants' response to this issue reveals that attitudes to self-censorship shape the experience of viewing violence to a substantial degree.

Boundary testing

The practice of thresholds and self-censorship highlights the way in which participants test boundaries whilst viewing violence. Boundary testing involves participants identifying a threshold of violence and choosing whether to self-censor or not. The way in which participants utilize this consumer choice is through anticipating and preparing for violent scenes to occur; participants anticipate a threshold whilst viewing violence and prepare for their choice of self-censorship. Although male and female participants perceive a difference between the way active consumers of violent movies test boundaries, anticipation and preparation are intrinsic to all participants, and boundary testing applies whatever levels of self-censorship are chosen.

Anticipation and preparation

Evidence from the focus groups suggests participants are aware of the role anticipation and preparation have to play in the process of viewing violence. One participant describes the effect of anticipation on the viewing process. He says: 'I have a harder time watching the build-up to violence than the actual incident. I get so tense. I don't mind the actual violence itself, it's the build-up to it; you can feel the fear in your seat' (Participant 3 – FG1). Another group member describes her response to the ear-amputation scene in *Reservoir Dogs*:

> This is one of the most disturbing scenes I've ever seen. The guy's completely defenceless, there's a knife, the atmosphere is completely electric. I looked up twice, once when he wiped the blood on his shirt, and once when the music came on because I felt relaxed. Then I felt the atmosphere again and I just didn't want to watch it. It has a horrible effect on me. (Participant 5 – FG3)

The way this participant describes her response to this scene highlights the close attention she pays to her own sense of anticipation. Because the cop is defenceless and there is a knife, this participant anticipates torture and therefore chooses to self-censor those moments in the scene she believes to contain representations of torture. She notes the atmosphere, and looks up to view the scene only when she anticipates the atmosphere has altered, i.e. the torture has ended. This example of self-censorship took place during a discussion group and this participant's body language was such that she showed her anticipation for the violence by covering her ears with her hands as the scene was screened.

Preparation follows anticipation when viewing violence. As this participant indicates, anticipation of a torture sequence in the film *Reservoir Dogs* leads to preparation of self-censorship: she looks away from the screen and covers her ears with her hands, a choice of self-censorship appropriate to the violence in this scene. With preparation comes a self-conscious awareness of the activity of self-censorship. When this participant was asked what she was thinking about whilst she was self-censoring the ear-amputation scene, she replied:

> I was thinking that I need to lose weight [she laughs]. I was thinking what are the others thinking about me? Am I over-reacting? Should I watch it? I felt my heart pounding. I could almost cry actually, that's how I felt. (Participant 5 – FG3)

This participant is very conscious of her own response to this scene and how other group members perceive her. She thinks of her physical appearance; she questions the intensity of her reaction; she focuses on her heightened emotions: her response reveals the vulnerability she feels whilst self-censoring, and her conscious awareness that other people will be watching her reaction to viewing violence.

Thus, anticipation and preparation are conscious activities which serve to highlight participants' awareness of other moviegoers. This awareness is most apparent when participants consider specifically male and female methods of self-censoring. In the next section, the way in which the issue of gender and the two factors of anticipation and preparation come together can be linked with perceived notions of male and female consumers of violent movies.

The issue of gender

Male participants perceive female consumers of violent movies to physically and vocally respond to representations of violence, and liberally self-censor, actions which male participants consider the opposite to their own non-responsive state when viewing violence. Female participants perceive male consumers of violent movies to brace themselves when representations of violence occur, and rarely, if ever, self-censor whilst viewing violence. As one participant explains: 'I don't want to be sexist but I know a couple of women who wouldn't like to watch these films. All the geezers I know feel "I'm too hard not to watch it", but women tend to react a bit more' (Participant 5 – FG1). Thus, participants perceive each other as anticipating thresholds of violence and preparing to self-censor, or not self-censor, depending on the gender of the viewer.

These different attitudes to self-censorship shape methods of use. For example, the majority of male participants claim they do not self-censor violent representations, even if they find the violence disturbing and it is identified as a threshold. Methods for not self-censoring centre around the two areas of anticipation and preparation. Most male group members prepare to sit through a violent scene in its entirety and one of the ways to prepare for viewing violence is to anticipate the worst and most violent scenario that could occur: thus when watching a scene, participants can imagine an act of violence far worse than is in actual fact depicted (see Chapter 4, 'The Activity of Viewing Violence', for further discussion). Participants may desire to self-censor, but by preparing properly this desire will not be acted upon. One participant comments:

> I sort of put myself through seeing a film to see if I can brave it. You know, everyone else has gone to see it and you're a wimp if you can't sit through it. Perhaps there are some things that make me nauseous, but I would try to watch it, I wouldn't cover my eyes, I would say: 'oh I've got to see this.' It's a bit like going to the dentist. (Participant 2 – FG4)

The description of going to the dentist is apt; most male participants view violence as if they have the drill in their mouth: to interrupt events may be fatal. Many male participants possess a serious attitude to viewing violence, they feel a responsibility to watch events, no matter if they find these events disturbing.

For some male participants this is an excuse for macho posturing. As the above example illustrates, phrases such as 'to see if I can brave it' and 'You're a wimp if you can't sit through it' signify the relevance of strength and endurance to some male participants' attitudes to self-censorship. Testing boundaries in this instance is about testing strength and endurance.

Other participants consider a non-responsive state desirable when viewing violence and this non-responsive state is part of testing boundaries. Two examples will illustrate this:

> You pay your money and you want to see the whole film. You may find certain things distressing but you still watch the film. (Participant 4 – FG1)

> I don't think I've ever looked away from anything. I just want to watch the film. I don't really take the violent aspect into consideration when

I want to watch a film, it's not something I think about. (Participant 3 – FG3)

These participants emphasize their non-responsive state when viewing violence; looking away, not watching a film, thinking about the violent content in a movie are all activities which these participants do not take part in. They perceive themselves as distanced from violent representations, and even though, as the first example reveals, these participants may find certain scenes disturbing, they choose to watch the 'whole' film rather than self-censor.

When asked why they did not wish to self-censor, comments indicated many male participants feel a duty to watch the 'whole' movie if they wish to take film, a form of art, seriously. Two participants explain:

I know people who react in different ways to violent scenes and I think it would be very wrong to get so far into a film and then go, 'no', and turn the film off. If someone wants to close their eyes during a scene fair enough but to just turn it off and say: 'oh no, that's too bad, I can't watch any more of it' is detrimental to an overall opinion of the film. You can't comment on something unless you've seen it all the way through. (Participant 3 – FG4)

You know a film's going to be bad, you think it's going to be bad but you watch out of respect for the art, I hope. You're preventing the film maker from presenting his message. The proper approach to art is one of humility and openness. Acting as a censor is a proud action not a humble action. (Participant 4 – FG1)

Both participants are adamant films need to be watched in their entirety, and violent movies are no exception. For the first participant, certain forms of self-censorship he has observed in others, not himself, are acceptable forms of behaviour when viewing violence, however to choose to switch off a film is a method of self-censorship which is perceived as unacceptable to this participant. Why this form of self-censorship is perceived as unacceptable can be related to the concept of watching the 'whole' film, signifying respect for the film maker: viewers cannot say they have seen a film if they have chosen such an extreme method of self-censorship. For the second participant, to not watch a violent film, even though the film may be 'bad', i.e. extreme, is an act of disrespect for the film maker, a proud action not a humble action. For this participant self-censoring is a form of sacrilege. What is common to both participants is an awareness that it is other viewers, not they, who self-censor. This is exemplified when the second participant replies to a comment that female consumers of violent movies over-react to scenes of violence. He says:

I took a woman friend to see one of these films and I couldn't tell her reaction. Well, her reaction was no reaction. She didn't move, I didn't hear her say anything, and she wasn't in a state afterwards. She was super cool. (Participant 4 – FG1)

Her reactions mirror this participant's own response to violence, i.e. no response, and this method of viewing violence is associated with male rather than female consumers of violent movies – it is 'super cool'.

For many male participants not self-censoring a violent scene or image is part of their interest in choosing to see violent movies in the first place. It is an enjoyable ordeal. Two participants comment:

> The worst thing I can remember doing is if a film gets really gross then maybe I'll look away, but there is that thing that you're still kind of curious. (Participant 1 – FG4)

> If I'm watching a film, I don't want to miss any of it. I'm aware that it's not necessarily the right thing to watch in terms of how it has an effect on me but I don't seem to turn away easily. (Participant 1 – FG3)

As these participants highlight, it is the challenge of viewing the 'whole' film which draws certain participants to not self-censor; they may desire to look away, but by anticipating violence they can prepare to test their own boundaries of response, to test endurance levels. This aspect of male participants' response to self-censorship serves to indicate that for some participants, to be desensitized to violent representations is not a negative reaction, indeed in many ways it is a desired reaction.

Sensitivity is a term applied to perceptions of female consumers of violent movies. Female participants provide examples of self-censorship where they have used anticipation and preparation to deliberately eschew specific types of fictional violence, and this is something male consumers of violent movies are perceived as unlikely to undertake. Two examples will illustrate this. One participant actively chooses not to watch horror films. She explains:

> I do self-censor. I don't go and see films like *Nightmare on Elm Street*. I find them quite scary and there tends to be a predominance of violence against women and I don't like that. I know a lot of people don't find them scary but I find them absolutely terrifying. I self-censor because I don't want to see women get it as victims. I went to see *The Shining* when I was quite young and this film scared me so much I just decided never to go and see another horror film. The thrill while you're in the cinema isn't worth the risk when you get home, when you can't sleep. And if you live on your own then you certainly don't need that kind of thing, you really don't need to feel that scared when you're at home. (Participant 3 – FG5)

This female participant identifies thresholds and uses self-censorship in a way which highlights her sensitivity to violence towards women. She is afraid of violence in real life and acknowledges that watching horror films where, as she puts it, 'women get it as victims', only serves to highlight the danger of violence for this participant: the 'thrill' of fictional violence isn't worth the 'risk' of real violence. Personal experience, reference to her fear of horror films, reference to her awareness of other moviegoers who are not disturbed by this type of violence are factors which indicate this participant has a low threshold for this type of violence and liberally self-censors in order to control her viewing experience. She does not test her response because she is aware of how fearful she will be if she watches horror films.

Another participant does not like to see violence towards women. She will not watch films which contain such representations because she fears the same violence may happen to her. She recalls watching *True Romance* and choosing to self-censor a specific scene because it contained violence towards women:

> In *True Romance*, when Alabama is fighting with that guy and she gets the corkscrew, I thought it was going to be a surprise and she was going to plunge it into his heart, but she stabbed him in the foot instead. I thought, oh no, he's going to rape her and she was in the bathroom with glass everywhere and I couldn't watch it after that. I didn't watch the rest of the film. (Participant 2 – FG3)

This participant anticipates Alabama (Patricia Arquette) will be raped and killed. She prepares herself for this event and self-censors, yet by self-censoring she is unaware that Alabama violently and successfully defends herself against her attacker. Therefore, this participant highlights her sensitivity to violence towards women in film by choosing to self-censor, but through doing so is not able to watch the 'whole' film and consequently does not realize Alabama is not raped and killed. For many male participants, this form of self-censorship would be a sacrilege, revealing a low threshold for violence and an inability to comment on the entire film. Once again, this participant does not wish to test her response because she is aware how disturbed she will be if a female character is raped and killed in a fiction film.

Participants' response to self-censorship and boundary testing so far reveals there is a perceived gender division in the way participants view violence. However, subtle variations and contradictions in participants' response to self-censorship indicates that the way participants perceive response is very different to the actuality of response to thresholds of violence. What can be seen is that participants borrow methods of response from what are perceived as traditionally male or female domains. Thus, participants undermine the gender division they themselves perceive, by reacting differently to the perceived notion of male and female viewing methods. What is more, all participants utilize context, characterization and the role of anticipation when choosing whether to self-censor or not, and these shared methods may be used to achieve different goals, but they also serve to highlight how similar male and female participants' response to violence can be.

For example, many male participants at first indicated they did not self-censor and wished to 'endure' fictional representations of violence. However, once this distinction had been made contradictions occurred within male attitudes to self-censorship. Once having stated: 'I do not self-censor' rare examples of self-censorship ensue: 'I do not self-censor, but there was this one occasion...' Two participants comment on rare instances of self-censorship:

> I went to see *Misery* and when James Caan's legs are broken it made me want to put my hands over my eyes. I watched it the first time, and when I knew she was going to hit him I put my hands over my eyes. What made me watch it again was to try and keep my eyes open the second time. (Participant 2 – FG1)

> The only time I would consciously glance away is if the violence is to do with the phallic – it just hits a spot, my crutch – but normally I try not to self-censor. I actually do prefer to watch and try to take on board the message of a film. (Participant 1 – FG6)

Here, these two participants identify thresholds and choose to self-censor. Both participants point out this is not a common occurrence; the first example emphasizes he watched the same scene again in order to test his own boundaries; the second example states that most of the time, apart from this exception, he will always watch a film in its entirety and 'try not to self-censor'. However, despite these considerations it is still possible to see how these male participants utilize elements of what is perceived to be female response to viewing violence.

This transference of methods can be found in female participants' response to violence. A number of female participants adopt what is perceived as specifically male attitudes to viewing violence. As one participant explains:

> I do try to make myself watch things. It's interesting to me why people don't watch violence. Why is it that men make themselves watch? I find I've got an element of that in my personality and I will force myself to watch things; it's kind of like a test. I'm a person who has a great need to know a lot of things. I try to watch because I need to know. (Participant 4 – FG3)

Another female participant comments on her desire to not self-censor violence:

> I can't think of anything that would make me say: 'No, I'm not going to see that' because it has something I don't like in it. I don't like eyes and injections, but I wouldn't turn away completely and I wouldn't not go and see a film just because I hear somebody gets their eye gouged out. Some films are really awful and I think I don't really want to watch any more of this, but I do try to stick with things, just so as I can talk about them. (Participant 1 – FG5)

As with male participants who admit instances of self-censorship, certain female participants utilize what are perceived as specifically male responses to viewing violence. These two female participants actively try to not self-censor because they wish to watch the 'whole' film, and even if they find certain representations of violence disturbing they will still try to test their own boundaries and steel themselves to watch fictional violence.

What these examples illustrate is the way in which male and female participants used similar methods whilst viewing violence. In order to not self-censor, participants must apply anticipation and preparation to the viewing process; similarly, in order to self-censor participants must apply the same devices: the goals may be different but both methods incorporate the same devices. What is more, in each instance boundary testing takes place; participants test individual response by choosing which level of self-censorship they wish to apply, and levels of self-censorship include watching and not watching violence. In the final section of this chapter male and female participants highlight the significance of boundary testing to the process of viewing violence.

Testing reactions

Evidence from the focus groups suggests there are three factors which are of significance to thresholds and self-censorship and the process of viewing violence. These factors are:

- Consumer Choice;
- Expectation;
- Boundary testing.

The function of thresholds and self-censorship is to utilize these three factors and test response to viewing violence. Whilst watching violent movies, participants identify individual thresholds, anticipate and prepare for these thresholds to occur, and choose whether to self-censor or not. It is through consumer choice that participants test boundaries.

A number of examples will serve to illustrate this. One participant actively self-censors, using all methods available. When watching the ear-amputation scene from *Reservoir Dogs* during the discussion, this participant forced herself to watch the scene a second time. She explains:

> When the scene started I thought, oh God, no I can't watch any of this, but because it wasn't the exact bit where the cop gets his ear cut off and I knew this wasn't for a while I watched the scene right up until Mr Blonde got the knife out and the music came on. Then, I thought, oh, this is the bit where I wouldn't watch last time. This time, I was sitting there thinking, oh no, but I carried on watching. I saw Mr Blonde stand in front of the cop and chop his ear off and I felt physically sick while he was doing it. I watched the bit afterwards when he talks into the ear. That was disgusting. But I think I was more disturbed the first time when I didn't see him doing it. (Participant 2 – FG3)

This participant tests herself to see how long she can watch this scene without self-censoring. She anticipates and prepares for the violence to occur, using her past knowledge of the scene to influence present viewing. Her reasons for doing this can be attributed first to the environment she is in; as part of a discussion group there is some pressure on her to watch the scene so that she can talk about it later. However, it is also clear from her body language and excited retelling of key stages in the scene that she gets a certain amount of satisfaction from testing her own thresholds with regard to violence. Each stage in the scene is accompanied by a testing of boundaries, and it is methods of self-censorship which aid this complex response.

As this example reveals, there is an excitement to be gained from boundary testing. Two participants comment:

> I love the thrill of daring yourself to watch a violent scene – that's a real kick. No, I'm not going to watch and then yeah, just do it, make yourself watch it. (Participant 7 – FG2)

> This year me and my friend have been boundary testing a hell of a lot and going to see films I've never wanted to see in my past life. I think: 'oh well, I can do this, and it's fine.' I'd say I've really changed and I've got a lot more open now and I'll see anything and see how it goes. (Participant 2 – FG5)

Both participants test their reaction to violent movies by daring themselves to watch scenes, or films, they would normally self-censor. In the first example, this participant feels there is a 'thrill' in persuading herself to watch something she expects to be disturbing; in the second example, there is a satisfaction to be had from changing consumer tastes, and being 'open' to seeing films this participant has never before wished to see.

The second participant goes on to explain the reason why she wished to watch violent movies and test her own boundaries. She says:

> A friend and I both ended five year relationships at the same time and were extremely miserable. I've always said I hate violent movies but I just thought, well, what the hell – I'll go and do something really horrible now because I want to counteract the relationship. So, for a four or five month stint we only saw violent films to prove we could do it. (Participant 2 – FG5)

Thus, personal experience can lead to an alteration in consumer tastes. This participant and her friend chose to view violent movies after long term relationships had broken down: violent movies, in this instance, act as a form of catharsis. As she explains:

> I wanted to see these films for my own benefit, you know, kind of use the system. It was very therapeutic. So with a long, particularly drawn out scene like the ear scene in *Reservoir Dogs* I say to myself: 'I will see this and I will get something out of it and I will test myself'. (Participant 2 – FG5)

This participant uses the process of viewing violence for her own benefit. She identifies the three areas the reactive mechanisms of thresholds and self-censorship are primarily concerned with: consumer choice; expectation; boundary testing, and relates these factors to her reasons for choosing to see violent movies.

It is the way in which participants utilize boundary testing that indicates there are strong similarities between the way male and female participants respond to violent movies. Whether self-censoring or not self-censoring, participants employ consumer choice, expectation and a desire to test individual response. Consumer choice signifies the methods by which participants choose to watch/not watch specific films or scenes containing violence; expectation signifies the way in which participants identify thresholds and choose to self-censor; boundary testing signifies a strong desire to monitor individual response when engaged in the social activity of viewing violence.

Conclusion

Boundary testing signifies consumer response to violent movies. There is no one method of self-censoring representations of violence, and participants utilize a range of methods from not self-censoring at all, to peeking through fingers, to eschewing specific types of violence altogether. Various methods of self-censorship are available because participants have complex and contradictory responses to viewing violence. Various methods of self-censorship are employed because participants' responses are fluid and dynamic. All methods of self-censorship are collateral with boundary testing, and it is here that participants indicate part of the reason for viewing violent movies is to test reactions to violence. Testing reactions is a way of interpreting response.

7

The question of entertainment

During the focus group discussions, participants considered the issue of real violence and fictional violence and the question of entertainment in relation to the target films. The emergent themes are as follows:

- Participants differentiate between real violence and fictional violence;
- Participants consider mediated images of real violence problematic in relation to their response to viewing fictional violence;
- Participants consider degrees of emotional involvement with real violence, mediated images of real violence and fictional violence central to their response;
- The term 'responsibility' and the role of 'witness' are significant to degrees of emotional involvement and response to viewing real violence, and mediated images of real violence;
- Participants consider real violence to be abhorrent and in no way entertaining;
- Participants consider the target films to be entertaining.

The above points signify that participants consider the issue of real violence, and mediated images of real violence a serious subject for discussion, and whilst they acknowledge that real violence can inform their response to fictional violence, they differentiate between the two media, and, significantly, perceive real violence to be abhorrent and not entertaining, whilst fictional violence is an acceptable form of entertainment. However, the term 'entertainment' is questioned, and participants consider there are different aspects of entertainment: those target films which are the most realistic are the least entertaining, whilst the target films which are the least realistic are the most entertaining. Thus, participants gauge their response to fictional violence according to an awareness of real violence. The ensuing sections present an analysis of these emergent themes.

Response to real violence

Real violence is raw

All participants clearly differentiate between real violence and fictional violence. Participants are deeply affected by real violence, whether they have been a witness to violence or experienced violence themselves. Two participants explain their response to real violence and mediated images of violence:

> If I see people fighting it upsets me more than anything I can tell you, more than anything I could ever watch at the cinema. I can't believe anyone is more sensitive to violence than I am in a real life situation. (Participant 1 – FG3)

> Real violence has a much more lasting impact. These are real people, that could have been a friend of mine, this could have been someone from my family, you know. I was thinking of some news footage of a massacre in Rwanda. That was much more shocking than these films. Real violence is really, really disturbing and really hard to take because it's so relentless. There are no clever one-liners, there are no little bits of humour to let you off the hook – the violence is raw. (Participant 1–FG4)

In both instances, each participant uses fictional violence to differentiate between the impact of real violence and viewing fictional violence: real violence is intense and shocking because it is real – it has a lasting impact, an impact fictional violence does not possess.

Participants do not find real violence, or mediated images of real violence entertaining. Many participants avoid watching news/documentary footage of violence and self-censor mediated images of real violence. One group member comments:

> There are certain things on the news I've avoided. When there was the Hillsborough disaster, the last thing I wanted to see was people getting crushed, it's not necessary. There are things like that I definitely avoid at all costs. (Participant 1 – FG3)

Participants point out real life experience of violence influences their response to fictional violence. For a few participants (detailed in Chapter 6, 'Thresholds and Self-censorship') this leads to active self-censorship of specific types of fictional violence, however for others it can highlight how unreal fictional violence is in comparison to personal experience of violence. One participant explains:

> Unfortunately, the lower down you are on the economic scale the more chance you have to witness violence whether you agree with it or not. You actually do witness the extent of violence and the damage it does, whereas the higher up the social ladder you climb the more likely you are to depend on the telly to portray what you accept as an image of violence. (Participant 1 – FG6)

For this group member, experience of real violence is linked to his social upbringing, and he claims such an upbringing brought him into contact with real violence, a contact which serves to highlight the unreality of fictional violence and mediated images of real violence. It is the 'extent' of violence and the consequences of violent acts which are significant to this participant; without knowledge of real violence, middle to upper class viewers 'accept' mediated images of real violence as real, when clearly, for this participant, this is not the case. Here, mediated images of real violence are implicitly criticized for their inability to show the consequences of first hand experiences of real violence, and the next sections explore this criticism in more detail.

Stylised news footage

Although real violence is considered extremely shocking, participants did not all agree that mediated images of real violence are dissimilar to viewing fictional violence. One similarity many participants consider significant is the film-like quality of mediated images of real violence. A number of comments will serve to illustrate this observation:

> The news is like a film sometimes, you just feel so detached, you feel nothing. (Participant 2 – FG3)

> I think there's a big grey area between so called fiction and so called real life. I find the so called real violence that you see on the news has a stronger effect than seeing someone's ear cut off in *Reservoir Dogs*. But that's another grey area, because the news is so sanitized and film violence is so stylized, and one of the techniques of film violence is to make it look realistic – it's very hard to tell. (Participant 4 – FG6)

> It seems to me that the media are playing with the image of screen violence. I thought the news footage of a woman holding her cat hostage and the American police shooting her dead was so unreal. It's manipulating the portrayal of real violence as entertaining and that's got to be worrying. (Participant 3 – FG4)

What participants highlight here, is an uneasy awareness of how news footage has influenced fictional representations of violence, and, vice versa, how fictional violence adopts stylistic features of mediated images of real violence. This perception of media representations of violence distances the viewer from the horrific impact of real violence. It has been mediated, and in a way familiar to consumers of violent movies.

Other participants comment on the way they feel desensitized to mediated images of real violence. One participant claims a direct relationship between his response to news footage of real violence and viewing fictional violence:

> I think the portrayal by the media of current events is what actually desensitizes ourselves to these target films and everything else as well. The news of the day is someone being shot through the head, or civil war in Africa. Even today, there was something on the news about some young children killing an old age pensioner and leaving him for dead in the gutter. You know about real violence, it's always happening. (Participant 2 – FG4)

Graphic images of violence on the news have become commonplace, and knowing about such graphic violence, watching the effects everyday, prepares this participant for viewing fictional violence: violent movies may be extreme, but real life can be far more horrific.

In the next section, participants reveal it is the impact of real violence and degrees of emotional involvement with this first hand experience of real violence, which is significant to their response to mediated images of real violence. If real violence is 'raw' and immediate, then violence on the news can appear distanced and unreal.

Emotional involvement

Participants' experience of different degrees of emotional involvement when viewing mediated images of violence and fictional violence is dependent on their understanding and experience of real violence. Real violence acts as an emotional barometer, and participants gauge their response to violence on the news, or a violent movie, by their understanding of real violence in contemporary society. One group member comments:

> Violence on the news doesn't have a physical impact. You think intellectually it has an impact. You think: 'oh shit, oh that's dreadful, that's a terrible tragedy.' But if you were actually involved in a real life situation, that has a concrete physical impact and you have a physical response to it in one way or another. (Participant 4 – FG3)

For this participant, degrees of emotional involvement are collateral with degrees of physical involvement when considering response to real violence, and violence on the news. First-hand experience of real violence ensures a 'physical impact', whereas mediated images of real violence attenuate the impact of violence for two reasons: a) it is mediated, and b) it is happening to someone else. Therefore, whilst some participants watch news/documentary footage of violence and imagine it could be them, or a loved one, in a similar situation, in order to experience a 'physical impact', other participants distance themselves from such emotional involvement by highlighting the lack of personal connection.

However, although all participants considered their experience of real violence as 'raw', and distressing, there was a distinction to be made between experiencing real violence and *witnessing* real violence. Some participants had *witnessed* real violence involving strangers, and found themselves strangely distanced from this experience of real life violence. One group member explains her complex response in some detail:

> When you're watching a film you get involved with the characters. If you see someone getting beaten up really badly in the street, I think, 'oh god that's really horrible', but when you see violence in the movies it's so much more intensified, things sound different and I think you come to accept them as more real. I go to any lengths possible to avoid violence. I managed to get through my whole senior school being in only one fight, the whole thing about people gathering round you terrifies me – it makes me feel sick right now. Yet, I can quite comfortably watch representations of violence in movies and even the news. I don't know if it's an empathy deficit but all you can think of is in theory and in the abstract: 'oh how awful it is for these people out there.' But, when you're watching a movie, you love this character, you just feel with them. (Participant 1 – FG5)

This participant presents a complex response to witnessing real violence, watching mediated images of real violence, and viewing fictional violence. She abhors real violence, yet, although disturbed by it, feels distanced and less emotionally involved when witnessing real violence in comparison to viewing fictional violence. When watching a violent movie, this participant builds character relationships and feels powerful emotional responses which she is not able to do to the same degree when considering real violence on the news or in real life. She empathises with characters because it is safe to do so; she accepts film violence as 'real' because it is safer to watch fictional violence than experience violence in real life.

Another example will illustrate this complex response to violence. This participant comments on the fact that violent movies can be more 'real' than watching mediated images of real violence. She says:

> The cinema is far more real than the news because you've built up an empathy with people and you give a shit. I mean, sometimes it's awful what you see on T.V but they cut so much out of it you don't actually see the awful stuff. (Participant 3 – FG5)

This participant claims mediated images of real violence appear abstract, whereas when viewing a film 'you give a shit' and become involved with character/s to a greater degree than is possible when watching the news. The significance of characterization is apparent here: it is emotional involvement which acts as a barometer to viewing violence (see Chapter 5, 'Building Character Relationships').

It is not only when watching the news that this participant feels detached from events taking place. She goes on to explain her response to witnessing real violence in relation to viewing violent movies:

> I've seen someone beaten up and stabbed outside my front door and that was less traumatic than seeing a character in a film, who you really care about and like, being beaten up. It was reality, yes. I did what you should do and called the police. But I didn't know that man. When I saw the man in court after the event and spoke to him, this was far more disturbing because I saw the scar and he was far more real to me than when he was outside my front door. (Participant 3 – FG5)

This participant differentiates between witnessing real life violence involving someone she does not know, and viewing fictional violence involving characters she does know. It is the degree of emotional involvement which is significant here. It is only once this participant comes face to face with the victim of the attack she witnessed outside her front door, and sees the consequences of this act of violence in the form of his scar, that she experiences a degree of emotional involvement. While the attack took place she was strangely distanced from this incident of real life violence.

Thus, from this participant's comments, it is possible to consider that fictional violence can signify a safe environment where high degrees of emotional involvement can be experienced, secure in the knowledge that this will have little effect on real life experience. Witnessing real life violence and viewing mediated images of real violence have less impact on this participant then watching fictional violence because she does not want to become emotionally involved with these real life violent events. As a consumer, she chooses to watch violent movies because they allow room for physical/emotional responses and character relationships which would be too painful to experience in real life.

Why this participant chooses to watch violent movies is explained when she comments:

> If you're living in the suburbs, violence does happen regularly in the pubs. Where I was brought up there was always violence on a Saturday night. So, if you want to avoid violence you come to London and you go to the cinema. Real violence is horrible but we'll go to the cinema to see it because it's a safe way. I avoid real violence at any costs, but I'll go and see violent movies because the violence isn't real. (Participant 3 – FG5)

This participant escaped small town violence by coming to the city, yet she chooses to watch films about violence because it is 'safe', it 'isn't real'. Therefore, although this participant wishes to avoid real life violence, and left her own suburban town in order to do so, she does not eschew all interest in violence. Her awareness of real acts of violence is transformed into a desire as a consumer to watch movies which depict fictional representations of violence.

The issue of witnessing real life violence signifies an important shift in viewing mediated images of real violence and fictional violence. When witnessing real life violence that does not involve someone they know, participants feel distanced from events, but also feel a moral responsibility to become involved. As one group member explains: 'When you see real violence in the street there's that responsibility thing that keeps you rooted. As much as you want to run off, you think I've got to do something here' (Participant 4 – FG5). As participants become involved in an incident of real violence this sense of distancing decreases. Similarly, when viewing mediated images of real violence, many participants claim they feel distanced from events: the violence is abstract because they cannot become involved. For those participants who wish to become involved, imaginative hypotheses occur – 'it could be me'- and this makes mediated images of violence more real, and therefore more disturbing because the participant has become an active witness.

However, if degrees of emotional involvement and the closeness of real violence can be charted here, the reverse takes place when considering fictional violence. When viewing fictional violence many participants claim they become more emotionally involved because the events taking place are fictional, i.e. distanced, and the cinema is a safe way of experiencing emotions they are unable to experience to the same degree in real life because it is separate from real life. This distinction is highlighted when many participants claimed they were more emotionally involved when watching *Schindler's List* (Steven Spielberg, 1993) than documentary footage of the holocaust. As one participant says:

> I've seen some documentaries that you just think are horrific. I think it's just like bearing witness. When *Schindler's List* came out it had some incredibly horrific footage, I mean it wasn't real, but I think it was one of the most traumatic things I've ever seen. (Participant 4 – FG5)

The holocaust is a real event, just as serial killers, domestic violence and gangsters are real, yet to see these events depicted as fiction enables participants to reach a level of emotional involvement they would not wish to experience in real life. There is a responsibility in watching certain types of fictional violence, but this is of a very different kind to the responsibility of witnessing violence in real life. One is a form of entertainment, the other a moral dilemma with dramatic repercussions for the individual.

This conscious awareness of real violence when viewing fictional violence is of specific interest when considering the question of entertainment. Evidence suggests that although participants differentiate between real violence and fictional violence, and do so in a number of varied ways, a conscious awareness of real violence when viewing fictional violence is present in each case. What is more, evidence indicates that it is precisely because participants abhor real violence that they choose to see violent movies. As one participant explains:

> When you're watching violent films they're just a safe way of experiencing the things you might be really, really frightened about in real life. I don't want to be beaten up, I'm scared of real violence, but I'm not as scared when I watch a violent film because I feel I can safely get out all my fears – it's a legitimate way for me to deal with violence. (Participant 1 – FG5)

How this connects with perceptions of entertainment will be detailed in the next section.

The safety of cinema

A number of issues emerged when participants considered the question of entertainment in relation to the target films. Participants regarded all of the target films as entertaining in a way real life violence and mediated images of real violence cannot be. However, once this distinction had been made between perceptions of entertainment and fictional versus real violence, participants openly debated the validity of the term 'entertainment'. Participants note different films are more entertaining than others and how they choose to define the term 'entertainment' depends on taste, individual preferences, critical appreciation, and stylistic representations of violence. A number of examples will serve to illustrate how participants debate the issue of entertainment:

> It depends on what you mean by entertaining. *Reservoir Dogs* I found entertaining because it was completely different to anything I'd seen before and quite exciting for all that, but at the same time quite disturbing and horrific. So, there was an entertainment side and another side which isn't what I'd call entertaining. *Pulp Fiction* I found thoroughly entertaining in every way. (Participant 3 – FG5)

> I think you would have to define what you meant by entertainment. I think in the old fashioned sense *Pulp Fiction* was the only film that I thought entertaining. I engaged with the other films on certain levels but I don't think I would use the word entertaining. There is entertainment that is disturbing and entertainment that is funny. (Participant 1 – FG4)

> There are different aspects of entertainment. I mean for me *Pulp Fiction* was fun, but *Henry, Portrait of a Serial Killer* – you haven't had a huge giggle watching it, but it's made you think a bit more. Participant 4 – FG6)

These three participants consider what the term 'entertainment' signifies for them. There are different aspects of entertainment; some movies are fun to watch, others are disturbing but can still be termed entertaining, and some films aren't entertaining at all, but can be considered thought provoking. Individual experience is significant and helps to define what participants consider to be, or not to be an entertaining violent movie.

This recourse to individual experience links with the reactive mechanisms of thresholds and self-censorship, discussed in Chapter 6. One participant defines which target films are entertaining by considering her role as a consumer. She says: 'I think *Reservoir Dogs, Pulp Fiction* and *True Romance* are entertaining because you can choose what sort of level you become involved in. I have a choice' (Participant 4 – FG5). Another participant examines the issue of thresholds and her role as a consumer:

> I find Tarantino and *Natural Born Killers* entertaining. My friend and I really liked *Natural Born Killers,* we even adopted the names of Mickey and Mallory for a while. Watching these films is something I did in defiance of what people thought I should be doing. Previously I'd seen cinema as an extension of reality and I didn't want to become involved in that, but now I'm prepared to see it because it's fiction and I want to test boundaries. It's good to see intelligent and constructive films which also include elements that I wouldn't normally have thought I wanted to see. I like the idea of questioning entertainment. What does it mean? Is it something that makes you think or feel in comparison with what's real and not real? Does it make you feel able to cope with more situations than you thought you'd be able to see? (Participant 2 – FG5)

Here, the reactive mechanisms of thresholds and self-censorship combine in a complex way to inform the question of entertainment. At first, this participant chose not to see violent movies because she thought this was an area she would not find entertaining: violent movies are 'an extension of reality' and she did not want to become involved in such an area of reality. However, through a desire to push boundaries and test perceived thresholds of violence, this participant alters her opinion and considers movies such as *Pulp Fiction,* or *Natural Born Killers,* entertaining because they are fictional representations of violence, not an 'extension of reality'. This participant transforms a fear of real violence into an enjoyment of fictional violence, and her enjoyment is defined by the very fact that she is surprised at her own response – viewing violence can be an entertaining experience.

Certain violent movies are clearly more entertaining than others and why this is so is closely linked to a conscious awareness of real violence. As one participant explains:

> I think *Reservoir Dogs* is very entertaining. I think *Pulp Fiction, True Romance, Natural Born Killers* and to an extent *Man Bites Dog,* except for the rape scene, are entertaining. *Henry, Portrait of a Serial Killer* and *Bad Lieutenant* I just think are so relentless I can't possibly find them entertaining in any way. I think they are good films, and have a lot to say about the nature of violence and our response to it but I wouldn't say I enjoyed them and I wouldn't encourage people to see them – I wouldn't say: 'oh yeah, if you want a nice, unchallenging Saturday night movie just go to the pictures and see these films'. (Participant 1 – FG5)

Pulp Fiction is entertaining because it is fictional and distanced from real violence by its stylistic presentation. Its very stylishness separates the film from other violent movies such as *Henry, Portrait of a Serial Killer*, *Man Bites Dog* and *Bad Lieutenant* because even though a film like *Man Bites Dog* is fictional it utilizes realistic devices, such as documentary style footage, which makes it appear real. The closer a fictional film comes to real images of violence, the more difficult it is to watch, and the less entertaining it appears to participants.

Here are three participants criticizing the realism of *Man Bites Dog*:

> I don't think *Man Bites Dog* is entertaining. It's done in black and white; it's sub-titled; it's French. It's just too realistic. It's depressing visually, and it's not Hollywood. (Participant 5 – FG3)

> The way *Man Bites Dog* is shot, the whole kind of documentary nature of it makes it hard to sit down and think 'oh, I'm really enjoying this film', someone's telling a story, and it's visually entertaining. It's not like that; it's not like your being told a story. I actually switched off for a while. I wasn't bored – the violence just didn't have an effect on me anymore; it was violence for it's own sake and it was trying to be more and more graphic each time, just to upset me. (Participant 1 – FG3)

> In *Man Bites Dog* there were some funny scenes, but there were bits that did get too much. Like the rape scene. I can see they're trying to have a joke and I just couldn't find it funny. It was too horrifying. It was a bit too much like a documentary, you couldn't really laugh at it. (Participant 1 – FG4)

These participants criticize the movie for its lack of narrative drive, its lack of Hollywood style, and its realistic depiction of violence. These are aesthetic and personal criticisms which draw upon an awareness of real violence to define what is not entertaining about this violent movie. The fact that participants continually refer to the way *Man Bites Dog* or *Henry, Portrait of a Serial Killer* appear too similar to viewing mediated images of violence is a clear indicator participants do not desire to be reminded of the horror of real violence. As one participant explains:

> When I watched *Henry, Portrait of a Serial Killer*, it wasn't so much the scenes themselves that I considered extremely violent, as the way in which they came across. I felt I had actually witnessed violence. Most other films the violence is glossed over, or done with a sense of humour to take the edge of it so that it doesn't leave you too shell-shocked. The thing is, if you actually see violence for what it is, it is horrific. (Participant 1 – FG6)

It is this sense of feeling shell shocked and the link with issues of realism and entertainment when viewing violence that will be of particular interest to further research in this area. Earlier in this section, participants reveal it is precisely because they abhor real violence that they choose to watch violent movies, and that a conscious awareness of real violence is central to the level

Figure 3: Man Bites Dog: 'Ben, the serial killer'

of emotional involvement available to participants. However, the safe, protective environment of a fiction film is only present when the film itself takes steps to distance the viewer from an awareness of real violence. Thus, aesthetic constructs such as characterization, dialogue, and the fictional style of a movie allow room for participants to feel safe, a central concept to the enjoyment of viewing violence.

Conclusion

Participants differentiate between real violence and fictional violence: real violence is raw, and considered not entertaining in any way. Mediated images of real violence are not considered entertaining, but are felt by some participants to imitate the stylised nature of certain violent movies. In some instances, this stylised presentation of real violence can distance the viewer from events taking place.

Levels of physical and emotional involvement are significant to how participants engage with real violence and fictional violence. Participants consider their experience of real life violence to have a serious physical and emotional impact on their lives. However, some participants who had witnessed real life violence towards people they did not know claimed to feel distanced and 'numb' to these incidents of real life violence. It is their lack of emotional involvement which produces this distancing effect. In contrast, fictional violence can engender high degrees of emotional involvement, precisely because it is divorced from reality.

Those films which underscore a fictional dimension, such as *Pulp Fiction*, or *Reservoir Dogs*, and have a specifically stylized representation of violence are more likely to be considered entertaining by participants because participants feel safe whilst viewing such films. Those films which underscore the non-fictional dimension, such as *Henry, Portrait of a Serial Killer*, or *Man Bites Dog*, and have a specifically realistic representation of violence are less entertaining because participants do not feel safe whilst viewing such films.

The safety of cinema is only applicable when participants feel they are watching a film, a fictional representation of reality. Real violence is an area all participants understand and do not wish to experience; fictional violence is a medium participants understand and enjoy. The way participants interpret fictional violence is through an understanding that it is not real. Thus viewers can feel free to explore a range of responses to viewing violence, safe in the knowledge that these responses are individual, and will not have repercussions in the real world.

8

Reservoir Dogs: A case study

Participants were shown the ear-amputation scene from *Reservoir Dogs* (Tarantino, 1992) during the focus group discussions. What follows is a case study of participants' response to this scene in the light of emergent themes discussed in the previous chapters. The purpose of this case study is to illustrate the complex and dynamic ways participants respond to violent movies. This case study is structured in five stages:
- Brief summary of the scene;
- A consideration of societal/cultural issues which effected participants' response;
- Analysis of participants' response to the two main characters in the scene;
- Analysis of response to audio/visual effects;
- An examination of the effects of repeated viewing and the cult status of this scene.

Summary of scene
Context
The context of this scene is as follows: a group of gangsters, only known as Mr White, Mr Pink, Mr Blonde etc. have taken part in a heist which has gone dramatically wrong. Those who have survived the heist meet at a disused warehouse. Whilst Mr Orange (Tim Roth), an undercover cop, lies bleeding to death from a gun shot wound, the others – Mr White (Harvey Keitel), Mr Pink (Steve Buscemi), Mr Blonde (Michael Madsen) – argue about their chances of survival, especially as Mr Blonde is known to the others as a psychopath. It is Mr Blonde who has captured a cop (Kirk Baltz), and brought him to the warehouse, like a cat returning with a bird. It is clear that the gangsters do not regard the cop as a human being, only a cop, someone who is a threat to their existence. As it turns out, it is the gangsters themselves who threaten their own existence. It is the arrival of the cop which prompts the beginning of the ear-amputation scene, and it is the cop who signifies the beginning of the end for the gangsters, who, one by one, kill each other in desperation to discover who betrayed the gang.

Ear-amputation scene
Mr Blonde (Michael Madsen) watches Mr White (Harvey Keitel), Mr Pink (Steve Buscemi) and Nice Guy Eddie (Chris Penn) leave the warehouse; Mr

Blonde is to stay with Mr Orange (Tim Roth) and the cop (Kirk Baltz). Mr Orange is bleeding to death on a ramp and the cop, taken as hostage by Mr Blonde, is tied to a chair and has been severely beaten. Mr Blonde takes off his jacket, utters the ominous words: 'Alone at last' and walks towards the cop. His first words to the cop come in the form of a joke: 'Guess what? I think I'm parked in a red zone.' Throughout this scene Mr Blonde laughs at his own jokes and often has a wry smile on his face, as if there is another joke we have not heard.

There is an interchange between Mr Blonde and the cop and we realize Mr Blonde will torture the cop for his entertainment, not to gain information. The scene takes shape; the cop's mouth is taped; Mr Blonde teases the cop with what he is about to do, pointing a gun at his head, dancing with a razor he will shortly use on the cop. Significantly, when Mr Blonde reaches inside his cowboy boot for the razor he asks the cop: 'Do you ever listen to K-Billy's Super Sounds of the Seventies?' The question leads to the external diegetic sound of the radio, and one song 'Stuck in the Middle with You'. It is during this song that Mr Blonde dances to the music then moves forward to slice the cop's ear off. As Mr Blonde leans forward to do this, the camera pans to the left and we do not see the ear being amputated. The camera remains for some time positioned in front of a ramp and an opening at the top of the ramp, above which reads a sign cautioning workers to 'Watch Your Head'. The sign, music and performance of Mr Blonde emphasize the humour in this scene, whilst the cries of the cop are real and painful to hear. The sequence ends when Mr Blonde makes a joke into the cop's severed ear, then throws the ear off screen and walks out of the warehouse, telling the cop: 'Don't go anywhere. I'll be right back'. (Tarantino, 1994a, pp.60-63)

Societal/cultural factors

The ear-amputation scene in *Reservoir Dogs* is both popular and infamous to consumers of violent movies. The scene has acquired cult status for a number of reasons: dialogue and soundtrack make the scene unusual; performances are memorable; direction is assured and thoughtful. What is significant in this study is the manner in which the ear-amputation scene embodies the issue of boundary testing: the scene is infamous because everybody knows someone who could not watch Mr Blonde torture Marvin.

Reservoir Dogs is a film which has attracted media attention for the way it tests boundaries. Distributers were hesitant about taking the film; people claimed to walk out of screenings, for example Wes Craven, the famous horror director (*Last House on the Left* [1972], *A Nightmare on Elm Street* [1986]) walked out of this film at a horror festival at Sitges.[1] Reviewers chose to emphasize its shocking and visceral content matter, with headlines such as 'Deadly Dogs Unleash a Whirlwind of Violence'(Usher [1992, p.26]), or

---

1.   See Nigel Floyd, 'Dog Days' in *Time Out*, 30 December 1992, where in an interview with Tarantino about *Reservoir Dogs*, Floyd refers to seeing Wes Craven, director of, amongst other films, *A Nightmare on Elm Street* (1984) walk out of a screening of this film at the Sitges horror festival, 1992. For an interview with Tarantino, discussing this furore over the ear-amputation scene, see Nilsson (1993) in *Samhain*, Issues 36 & 37, Jan/Feb, Mar/Apr 1993, pp.12-15, pp.12-13. And Church 1993, 'Colours on the Charnel House' in the *Observer*, 8 January 1993. See also Middleton (1995) in *Samhain*, Issue 50, May/June, 1995, p.7, for an interview with Lucio Fulci (the famous Italian horror director) where they discuss Carlo Rambaldi (a special effects man who worked with Fulci) walking out of this film because he found it too real.

'Shooting the Dogs of Gore' (Walker [1992, p.43-44]), and adverts played on its 'awesome, pumping powerhouse of a movie' reputation.[2] The BBFC chose to withhold *Reservoir Dogs'* video release in the wake of the *Child's Play III* furore.[3] When it was finally released on video, in June 1995, some journalists thought it should only be seen 'by consenting adults, in public', lest it unleash itself on the general public, 'like one of the hoodlums that it portrays' (Lisle [1995, p.27]).[4]

It is the ear-amputation scene in particular which has become a cultural magnet for media headlines and promotional gimmicks. For example, Derek Malcolm, in the *Guardian*, warns readers about the ear-amputation scene: 'There is a point in *Reservoir Dogs* when it is difficult not to take the ultimate sanction against violence and walk out' (Malcolm [1993a, p.6]); whilst Shaun Usher in a similar vein, discusses the ear-amputation scene at the start of a piece for the *Daily Mail* as follows: 'Steel yourself, for this is even more shocking to read than witness...' (Usher [1992, p.26]). One headline for an interview with Tarantino, promoting his new movie *Pulp Fiction* (1994), capitalized on the widespread fame of the ear-amputation scene: it said 'Killing Joke ... is *Pulp Fiction* ... the greatest thing since sliced ears?',[5] whilst a *Reservoir Dogs* stamp collection sports a picture of Mr Blonde pointing a gun in our direction – the text by his side tells us he doesn't 'give a XXXX.'[6]

Consequently, media hype and peer pressure ensure heightened levels of anticipation before and during the screening of this film. One participant describes his response on first watching the ear-amputation scene:

> The whole point to *Reservoir Dogs* was how violent it was and everyone kept going on about the scene where Mr Blonde chopped the cop's ear off. The minute the cop's sitting in the chair it is obvious that this is the scene where it's going to happen...I was expecting this. And I saw less than I thought I was going to see. I wasn't disappointed because I don't particularly want to see someone get their ear chopped off – but I thought it was milder than it was going to be. (Participant 1 – FG3)

Another participant discusses her anticipation and awareness of this scene through listening to the soundtrack, purchased before viewing the film:

> I thought the scene was incredibly intense. I found it disgusting and disturbing and quite upsetting. But that Tarantino humour creeps in. I've listened to the soundtrack of *Reservoir Dogs* so many times, you

---

2. Quotation by Neil Norman of the *Evening Standard* and displayed on cinema and video posters for *Reservoir Dogs*.

3. There were several reports of this in the press. For example, see Bateman, 1993. 'Dogs Impounded as BBFC shows teeth', *Screen International*, Friday 2 April 1993, p.6. French, S, 1993. 'Cut and Run is Wrong' in the *Observer*, 18 July 1993, p.53. See also, Ferman, 1994, 'At the Sharp End', *Empire*, no 59, May 1994, p.90 – see also pp. 84-91 for a more widespread reaction to the 'violent movie debate'.

4. For two opposing views of *Reservoir Dogs* video release, see Tim de Lisle, 1995, 'An Unhealthy Intimacy With Violence' in the *Independent on Sunday*, 11 June 1995, p.27, for an argument against, and Sean French, 1993, 'Cut and Run is Wrong' in the *Observer*, 18 July 1993, p.53.

5. Andrew (1994), *Time Out*, 21-28 September 1994, p.24.

6. These 'cut out and keep' stamps regularly appeared in *Time Out* as a promotional gimmick advertising *Reservoir Dogs*, and coincided with the promotion of *Pulp Fiction*. See for example, *Time Out*, 21-28 September, 1994 no.1257, 1994.

know, it was sort of going on in my head – I was listening to the sound
and tapping my foot. I like the way Tarantino juxtaposes those two
things. Extreme violence and then this snappy little song going on in
the background. (Participant 4 – FG3)

The reference to the successful soundtrack for *Reservoir Dogs* is another significant factor in participants' response to this scene. The song this participant
is referring to, Stealers Wheel's 'Stuck in the Middle with You', is a relatively
little known seventies pop song, yet, due to the popularity of the movie and
its related soundtrack, the song which accompanies the ear-slicing sequence
has become famous for its violent association in the movie. This is another factor in heightening moviegoers' anticipation of this scene before they have even
viewed the film. Indeed, there were even related soundtracks, such as one
titled *Abattoir Dogs* which came free with *Vox* magazine which capitalized on
the long running success of the *Reservoir Dogs* soundtrack released in 1992.[7]
Bars, restaurants and radio popularized this soundtrack, in particular the song
'Stuck in the Middle with You', and ensured many first time viewers of
Reservoir Dogs were already familiar with this song and its role in the ear-
amputation scene.[8]
So popular was this scene in the group discussions that participants often
discussed the ear-amputation scene as if it existed separately from the rest of
the film, and although references are made to other scenes, those scenes were
not integral to discussion of the ear-amputation scene: it existed as a subject
in its own right. Considering that later scenes include the death of Mr Blonde
and Marvin, it is interesting how little participants felt the need to refer to
other scenes in the film. This is another indication the ear-amputation scene
has acquired cult status: its infamous reputation for testing boundaries make
it the most popular scene to be discussed by group members.

Mr Blonde
Many participants consider Mr Blonde to be an attractive character. He is cool
and good looking; he has the best lines in the scene, and, most importantly,
he has a sense of humour. Significantly, in *Thelma and Louise* (Ridley Scott,
1991), the same actor (Michael Madsen) plays a likable, non-violent character and some participants recall this other character whilst Mr Blonde tortures
the cop. Therefore in the ear-amputation scene character and actor merge, but
participants are aware of this conflation and are also aware their attraction to
Mr Blonde/ Michael Madsen is both playful and fantastical. As one participant explains:

I love Michael Madsen. I think he's brilliant. I mean he always plays
some kind of psycho, but there's something about that I can't help
finding attractive – which is a scary thing to admit. In *Reservoir Dogs*
he is so totally wired and so totally weird and he's so far removed from
what happens in my everyday life that there is something slightly
attractive about that. (Participant 4 – FG3)

---

7.   Compiled by Roy Carr and Ace Records, 1995.
8.   Mark Kermode points out a similar phenomenon with the release of the soundtrack for *Pulp Fiction*,
     which was an even bigger best-selling soundtrack than *Reservoir Dogs*. See Mark Kermode, *Sight and
     Sound*, February 1995, p.62.

Figure 4: Reservoir Dogs: 'Mr Blonde'

Another participant comments on Mr Blonde's appearance:

> You imagine someone in a suit to be an intelligent, professional person and it doesn't go with his behaviour and that's attractive. The fact that he's wearing a white business shirt – it's like a wolf in sheep's clothing. (Participant 5 – FG3)

Participants comment on the attractiveness of Mr Blonde both despite and because of his violent and sadistic nature. It is his personality and appearance which count but, at the same time, his aggressive actions define aspects of his personality and appearance. One participant comments:

> Mr Blonde is so cool – and he's just about to do something disgusting. I'm glad you don't see him chopping the ear. I really feel sorry for the cop, but I don't care. I still like Mr Blonde. It doesn't change what I think about him. (Participant 3 – FG2)

This participant is attracted to Mr Blonde because he is "cool", but she also empathises with the cop; her way of dealing with this dual engagement is to focus on the fact that Mr Blonde is not shown cutting the cop's ear off – the distancing technique used in the film is also used by this participant in order to engage with the character of Mr Blonde.

It is precisely because Mr Blonde is a fictional character that participants identify those attributes they admire – his clothes, hair style, wry smile – as real details. Participants augment the character of Mr Blonde by focusing on these details. The details help create a relationship between Mr Blonde and the viewer, yet the substance of Mr Blonde, his violent nature, distances the viewer and is an important reminder: because this character is a fantasy it is safe to be attracted to him.

Some participants could not relate to this attraction for Mr Blonde, and questioned those participants who stated as such. Amongst female participants, the discussion remained light hearted, however, for male participants the issue was seen as more serious. In comparison to women, fewer men openly stated they were attracted to Mr Blonde; when such statements were made these men were asked to defend themselves. For example, one male participant comments : 'The humour almost makes you identify with Michael Madsen for some reason – maybe I'm a psychotic killer or something' (Participant 3 – FG6). This participant's tone suggests he is aware of the contentious statement he has made; the nervous reference to what he fears other participants may be thinking is emphasized in the throwaway phrase 'maybe I'm a psychotic killer or something'. Another group member follows this by stating: 'I don't know how you can say that' (Participant 2 – FG6), and the first participant is drawn into a discussion whereby he defends his response within the context of the film. Mr Blonde is a character, not a real sadist and as another participant points out: 'You wouldn't want to know any of these people, but in terms of watching the film I think it's quite legitimate to like them, or find them attractive in some way' (Participant 1 – FG5).

This difference in response to the character of Mr Blonde serves to highlight that although some participants do not engage with the character of Mr Blonde, other participants do so with full knowledge that this engagement is a safe way of experiencing danger, power and aggressive sexuality: no participant wants to be Mr Blonde, but through personal preferences and character augmentation they can build a relationship which is fictional and safe.

Marvin

In contrast, the actor Kirk Baltz is unknown, and most participants do not even refer to his character as Marvin Nash, but as 'the cop', even though his name is clearly stated when Marvin and Mr Orange talk after the death of Mr Blonde. The cop is a clever piece of casting as his good looks signify innocence and familiarity, he looks like anyone, the exact opposite to Mr Blonde who is handsome and sinister, a face to remember. One participant recalls viewing this film with her twelve year old daughter who refused to watch this scene because the cop had a nice face. She says: 'My daughter would not watch that scene simply because she thought: I'm not watching it, the policeman looks too nice, he looks like a man I know' (Participant 4 – FG2). Many participants empathize with the cop, but he is a symbol rather than an individual: he looks too nice to be sexually attractive, and is too nice to present a challenge to Mr Blonde.

Some participants respond in an emotive way to the cop's situation, often touching their ear when the torture sequence occurs. One participant comments: 'The cop doesn't have anyone to defend him; he hasn't got anyone to feel sorry for him, not even the audience' (Participant 3 – FG5). This participant assumes audiences will engage with Mr Blonde in this scene, and she empathises with the cop because he has no one to defend him. Thus this participant builds a character relationship based on contextual information in the scene itself, and imaginative hypothesizing outside of the scene: the cop has no one to defend him in the warehouse and no one to defend him in the cinema.

Evidence suggests that whilst participants are attracted to Mr Blonde, they also feel sympathy for the cop and try to imagine what he feels in this situation. Participants do not necessarily take sides, and whilst they may be more attracted to one character than another this does not lead to the exclusion of sympathy or understanding for all other characters. Two participants explain:

> The most disturbing thing about this is that the cop can't scream, you hear these – I don't no how to describe it – animal noises. Mr Blonde is just making a mockery out of him. And you have this mixture of feeling for the cop but at the same time you're laughing with Mr Blonde. I feel quite guilty. He's so horrible, but he's so funny. (Participant 4 – FG5)

> The young cop, he's only been on the force eight months and he doesn't know much, so you see him as a kid, and I feel for him because he's a victim in this thing. But then again, there's something about the humour of Mr Blonde which I kind of like. It's confusing, it really is. (Participant 3 – FG6)

The first participant is disturbed by the visual effect of the cop's mouth being taped up, and the noises he emits provoke feelings of sympathy for the victim. However, the humour of Mr Blonde is also amusing and counteracts the horror of the cop's situation. The second participant emphasizes those elements

Figure 5: Reservoir Dogs: 'Marvin, Mr White and Mr Pink'

of the cop – his youth, his innocence – which aid character engagement, yet he also acknowledges the humour of Mr Blonde, and highlights his own personal preferences – it is a humour he likes. Both participants feel sympathy and admiration for both characters at the same time and whilst they feel guilty and confused by this they nevertheless experience a variety of responses to both characters.

An awareness of the roles each character represents in the community, i.e. gangster and cop, can have an effect on viewer response. Some participants do not feel a great deal of sympathy for the cop precisely because they perceive the police as bullies and psychopaths. Thus real experience becomes a significant factor in the way participants build character relationships. One participant points out, if you sympathize with the gangsters and want them to succeed, then you may legitimately feel antagonism towards the cops whilst also empathizing with Marvin as an individual. She explains:

> When Mr Blonde slashes his face you know how much that must hurt, just think of the nick of a knife, you can tell how much agony he's in. In a way it is so complex because many people seeing that film are going to be quite happy to see a police officer in that situation, to be honest, and by now you've kind of grown to like the Michael Madsen character. Obviously he's psychotic but you know you have some kind of feeling for him – I know I did. (Participant 1 – FG5)

Another participant considers the scene as a role reversal of many instances where the police torture criminals:

> If you look at Mr Blonde he actually looks like a police officer – you know, the white shirt, the strides, the gun holster. To me it was like a role reversal. The difference is, the police officer would want the information but Mr Blonde says: 'I don't really give a shit'. He tapes the cop's mouth up to prove it... I can't say I identify with Mr Blonde but I don't like the police. I suppose to me the police are just there to repress individuals. When I was a teenager they treated me as if I was some sort of inferior being. (Participant 1 – FG6)

Both participants draw on personal experience to aid understanding of characterization. For one participant, negative experiences of the law ensure he has little sympathy for the cop; for another participant the experience of cutting herself with a knife engenders sympathy for the cop, despite her attraction to Mr Blonde. Both participants draw on personal experience whilst using aesthetic constructs within the movie to highlight such understanding; reference to Mr Blonde's clothes, his method of restraint, the cop's clothing substantiate the way in which these participants perceive characterisation in the ear-amputation scene, yet personal experience is also utilized in order to understand the politics of the scene, and, in this instance, negative experience or perceptions of the police influence character engagement.

Therefore, response to fictional characters in the ear-amputation scene is based on a fiction which is informed by real issues. Real details such as experience of the law, cutting oneself with a knife, having a nose bleed, merge with aesthetic considerations, such as the use of dialogue, mise-en-scene, casting and performance, to create a complex and informed response to the ear-amputation scene. Participants build character relationships by using a variety of methods, and their response is both dynamic and fluid.

Audio/visual effects

The ear-amputation scene involves a number of different stylistic features which aid the representation of violence. Participants highlight specific audio and visual effects which they consider instrumental in their response to this scene. There are two significant audio effects: the use of external diegetic soundtrack, in this instance the song 'Stuck in the Middle with You' by Stealers Wheel, and the muffled cries of the cop (Kirk Baltz) as he is tortured by Mr Blonde (Michael Madsen). For participants, the most significant visual effects are where Marvin bleeds through his nose whilst his mouth is taped, and where the camera pans to the left censoring Mr Blonde's sadistic act of violence.

Participants claim the song 'Stuck in the Middle With You' is both humorous and unsettling. Two participants comment:

> I've listened to the music on CD and I really like this song, but I also think: 'here's blood and chopped off ears, what a shame'. (Participant 2 – FG3)

> As soon as the music comes on you tap your toe – my god did I do that – when I'm absolutely disgusted with what's going on. (Participant 2 – FG2)

The music counteracts the acts of violence in this scene; when Mr Blonde dances to the rhythm it is comical to see such a violent man be so playful, yet participants are also horrified that the music is enjoyable and they are drawn to its rhythm.

The muffled cries of the cop (Kirk Baltz) counteract the singalong atmosphere. His mouth is taped, his hands are tied and his cries are audible, but distorted. Participants empathize and imagine what the cop's cries would sound like if his mouth was free. In many ways this is thought to be one of the most distressing parts of the sequence precisely because the victim's pain is repressed. Two participants comment:

> I looked up when the music was playing; the policeman was looking up and blood was dripping down on the tape and he was completely powerless in every sense, he couldn't voice his pain, he couldn't reason with Mr Blonde. He didn't even have the power of speech, he had nothing. He was just hearing and seeing and his eyes were so wide. (Participant 5 – FG3)

> I thought the most disturbing part of that scene is where they've got the close-up of the guy's face, the guy can't breathe, he's coughing up blood, its coming out of his nose. (Participant 1 – FG3)

The first participant self-censors during this scene, but is drawn to look up when she hears the music begin. She considers the visual and aural effect of the cop's taped mouth disturbing because he is 'completely powerless', he cannot 'voice his pain'. She anticipates the torture which will take place later because the cop is portrayed as so helpless at this moment. For the second participant, the sight of blood choking the victim once again signifies the cop's inability to express himself except in the most abject way and this emphasizes weakness and enables this participant to anticipate worse deeds to come.

Anticipating worse acts of violence prepares participants to choose various methods of self-censorship. Three examples will illustrate this:

> When I went out of the room I was thinking about the poor man struggling, and I couldn't imagine what Mr Blonde was going to do to him. (Participant 2 – FG3)

> I think this scene is disgusting. I saw it on video and I turned it off. I just don't like it. (Participant 4 – FG4)

> I'm glad the camera looks away and you don't actually see what's happening, but then again you have this curiosity. You don't want to see what he's doing but you want to know how it happened. (Participant 3 – FG6)

The first participant uses mental and physical barriers whilst self-censoring: she walks out of the room and concentrates on the cop's pain in order to not anticipate what Mr Blonde will do to him. The second participant turns off the video in no uncertain terms, whilst the final example half watches the ear-slicing sequence, relieved the film does not show the violent act but curious as to what is happening off screen.

It is the build-up of anticipation and a desire to test boundaries which is significant to participants' response to the visual effect of the ear-slicing sequence. Participants anticipate and prepare for extreme violence. One group member comments:

> It's obvious something is going to happen because of the tape on the guy's mouth. He doesn't do anything for two minutes, you know, he tunes the radio, building suspense. The whole thing is about this enormous difference in power; its got you on the edge of your seat. How far is this guy actually going to go before he does something? 'I'm going to kill you, but it can wait.' You get upset for the cop but you also think this is fantastic. (Participant 1 – FG3)

It is this build-up to the ear-slicing sequence which creates a sense of anticipation so great many group members believe they see the ear being sliced. For example, one participant thought he had seen the visual effect of the ear being sliced the first time he saw *Reservoir Dogs*, and believed the screening at the discussion was an edited version of the film he saw at the cinema. His cognitive response the first time he viewed this scene ensured he anticipated Mr Blonde's actions to such an extent he did not register the director's censorship. He says: 'I thought when you saw the scene you saw the ear coming off. I don't actually remember that pan across, strangely enough' (Participant 1 – FG4).

A later shot of the cop's head without an ear becomes confused with this earlier shot where the camera pans away and does not show the act of violence taking place. Even though participants are aware of this, they still express their surprise. One participant comments:

I guess I thought I saw more because I was looking at it through my fingers; I'm sure I didn't watch that scene in full – it was too much for me. But I don't remember them panning away. For me it was very vivid that he cut his ear off. So, really it didn't matter how the film was made; the fact is I saw his ear getting cut off and I was very disturbed by it at the time. (Participant 3 – FG5)

This participant indicates anticipation of violence is a strong cognitive process, and, once anticipated, cannot be dispelled easily from this viewer's mind. For this participant, her desire to test boundaries is such that her imagination creates an image of the torture taking place which is stronger than the actual sequence of shots on screen. What is more, self-censoring the scene means this participant has created two barriers to the viewing process: one mental, the other physical and she uses these to interpret the violence taking place.

As this example illustrates, the build-up of anticipation in this scene and its ability to test boundaries are so well orchestrated that some participants wish to see the visual effect of the ear-slicing. They expect to see it, and then to be deprived of this image creates even more feelings of disquiet. Indeed, many participants debate whether it is worse to not see the full effect of Mr Blonde's torture. It is worse because the act of violence becomes part of their imagination. A number of examples will illustrate this:

I found the scene quite gross. It was disturbing because they didn't actually show the act of violence. I always find my imagination is more disturbing than what anyone can show me on screen. I'd rather see Quentin Tarantino's imagination. My own imagination can be far worse. (Participant 4 – FG3)

I think this scene is really, really disturbing. And it's a lot worse that we don't see the cutting of the ear because it leaves it up to you to imagine that. It's really scary. (Participant 1 – FG2)

When the ear was being cut off and the camera pans away that action made me cringe more than if I'd seen the ear cut off. He slashes the cop's face which you see, but when the camera pans away and you don't know exactly what he's going to do, you worry and think what the hell is he going to do now. (Participant 2 – FG4)

Each example highlights the role boundary testing has to play in the process of viewing violence; it is because these participants anticipate extreme violence, and imagine something far worse than is shown on screen that they find this scene disturbing. Here, anticipation and preparation create individual experiences which are outside the framework of the film. Participants prepare for the impending torture in this scene by imagining the worst that could happen, and when they are not shown a scaled down version of their imagination on screen participants are left with disturbing images which cannot be easily dispelled. In this instance, testing boundaries involves participants' imaginative thresholds as well as textual thresholds.

Context is very significant to participants' reactions to representations of violence. In this instance, participants expect to see the ear cut off because they have heard so much about this scene through the media and friends. Certainly, participants claim when they first saw this scene they expected to see the act of violence in its entirety precisely because it was so infamous. This heightened level of expectation means certain participants were unaware of details in the scene which counteract their individual expectation. However, other scenes in this film and other violent movies do not necessarily produce similar results. It is the context of this scene and its utilization of boundary testing which creates this phenomenon.

Effects of repeated viewing

Repeated viewing leads to participants being more aware of aesthetic constructs (direction, acting, music) in the ear-amputation scene. Whereas first viewing highlights emotional response, repeated viewing highlights critical response. Two participants comment:

> It's the one scene in *Reservoir Dogs* I remember most vividly, but I was surprised when I watched it again that I laughed more: now, when I realize just how horrible it is I anaesthetize myself to it. (Participant 4 – FG5)

> Maybe it's because I'm concentrating on Mr Blonde and thinking, 'oh what a funny guy', or whether I'm concentrating on the camera angle, I don't know, but the ear-slicing scene no longer bothers me in the slightest. (Participant 3 – FG6)

These two examples highlight further instances of boundary testing. It is through repeated viewing that participants can test their initial response to the ear-amputation scene: part of the reason both these participants wish to see the scene again is to discover whether they will have a similar reaction. The 'test' concerns emotional and critical responses, and the desired result of this example of boundary testing is to not be as emotionally disturbed by this scene in comparison with previous responses. Here, the results of the 'test' show boundaries have shifted.

In the case of the ear-amputation scene, the deliberate use of music, humour and dialogue provide repeated opportunities for viewers to detect aesthetic constructs they are unaware of at earlier screenings: thus participants are able to shift from emotional to interpretive perspectives. One participant comments:

> I've seen this scene before, so this time I found myself concentrating on other things. Before I didn't notice the music at all, so this time I listened to it and I lost some of the impact of the violence by doing it. I also noticed how comical the scene was, how it tried to play the violence down by making it light hearted. So, most of the violence was lost on me because I was concentrating on other things. (Participant 3 – FG3)

As this example highlights, some participants consider their response to be different on repeated viewing. In this instance 'different' signifies less disturbed, and more attentive to aesthetic constructs, in particular the use of humour. Two other group members explain their change in response on repeated viewing:

When I first saw this at the cinema I felt nauseous. I think it would make anyone feel nauseous really. But having watched it a few times now I could eat a chocolate gateaux I'm so familiar with it. (Participant 2 – FG4)

The first time I saw it I was absolutely terrified. I wasn't expecting the violence. When Mr Blonde gets the knife out of his boot you think he's going to be chopping something off, but the ear is the last thing you think of. Now, I find this funny. (Participant 4 – FG5)

Once again, the ability to anticipate and prepare for the violence in this scene means participants can test boundaries and concentrate on details they were unaware of on first viewing: their response is critical rather than emotional.

However, it would be wrong to suggest participants only possess one method of viewing this scene at a time: both emotional and critical perspectives can be adopted at the same time, producing conflicting and varied results. This can entail emotive response to the representation of torture, and critical distancing to attenuate such emotional response: a form of self-censorship many participants adopt when they consider a representation of violence disturbing. Repeated viewing serves to reduce emotional response in this scene, but not necessarily to the extent all participants claim to be desensitized to the images. As one participant points out:

You go and see a film like *Reservoir Dogs* and I don't feel desensitized to it because the violence is dealt with in such a way it looks like it hurts. So, it still strikes me every time I see it how painful it is. (Participant 1 – FG5)

Other scenes which contain violence will not elicit the same response, and as participants point out, if violence is depicted as shocking then the viewer will not forget such a response even if they choose to highlight other aesthetic areas of interest when viewing a second or third time. Hence, participants who believed they saw the ear being sliced in *Reservoir Dogs* did not considerably alter their shocked response to this scene; they altered their attention to other areas of interest. The desired result of boundary testing can be to reaffirm initial emotional responses, whilst also highlighting critical responses on repeated viewing.

Levels of anticipation and adrenalin do alter considerably on repeated viewing, but this does not imply the viewer is desensitized, only more critically aware of representations of violence. Why participants wish to watch this scene over and over again, elevating a scene to cult status, can be attributed not just to boundary testing, but to how entertaining participants consider this scene to be. Indeed, the two are interlinked. Two group members explain:

I spent the whole time thinking I wonder if it will upset me like it did the first time. But it didn't. I thought it was a fantastic scene, one of the best I've seen in any film. (Participant 1 – FG3)

To be brutally honest I've seen that scene so many times now and I just think the dialogue is good, the direction is good, it's a really superb piece of filming. But it still shocks me. (Participant 3 – FG4)

Participants wish to view this scene again because they enjoy it. They praise the dialogue, individual actors, direction and soundtrack, not merely the representation of violence. It is a culmination of these aesthetic constructs within the context of the film, and the opportunity to test response on repeated viewing, which ensure the durability of this film's entertainment value.

Thus, the ear-amputation scene provides a number of different emotional and critical responses, which transform and in some cases increase on repeated viewing. Through repeated viewing, the ear-amputation scene provides opportunities to test boundaries and interpret and understand a scene whose subject matter is taboo and whose cult status ensures discussion at individual and social levels.

Conclusion

Participants are very aware of the ear-amputation scene and its infamous depiction of violence; they anticipate and prepare for viewing this scene knowing it represents a famous threshold. But, this does not mean participants only enjoy watching this depiction of violence, they respond to the context of the scene as a whole. Characterization highlights how important it is for participants to utilize personal experience and imaginative hypothesizing and engage with characters: what participants do not do is 'identify' with either Mr Blonde or Marvin, but build character relationships, drawing upon aspects of both characters in order to interpret violence.

Participants are aware of aesthetic constructs and how significant these are to their response to viewing violence: it is the audio and visual effect of Mr Blonde slicing the cop's ear off which activates physical and emotional response and methods of self-censorship. What is entertaining about this scene is not its graphic depiction of violence, but its clever dialogue, direction, and acting and the way it encourages critical and emotional responses. What is significant about this scene is the way viewers interpret the violence by testing boundaries. This is why many participants choose to view this scene a number of times.

This case study marks the end of the data analysis arising from the focus group discussions. It serves to highlight the significance of anticipation and preparation, character engagement, thresholds and self-censorship, and the issue of entertainment in relation to viewing violence. Central to these reactive mechanisms is the practice of testing boundaries – a process which is complex and dynamic and necessary to interpreting fictional representations of violence.

The final chapter in this study attempts to summarize this data and clarify the significant points to emerge from the research so far. This summary and conclusion will situate the results of this research in a wider perspective, and refer to other studies conducted in this area, although this is by no means meant as a 'review' of the literature in this field. What I hope to achieve in the conclusion to this book is a sense of how a theory of 'portfolios of interpretation', a theory which arises from the data analysis, can aid our understanding of the process of viewing violence. This theory is offered as a working model, not a fixed finding, and should prove useful to those who are interested in the phenomenon of violent movies.

9

Summary and conclusion

Contexts

The nature of qualitative research is that it provides a small-scale, in-depth examination of why people think as they do. The object of this study is to provide an examination of why people watch violent movies, and to explore the process of viewing violence. This study does not attempt to undertake a theoretical examination of the issues raised from the focus group discussions because this is a subject for further research. *Shocking Entertainment* presents un-'theorized' data in order to provide the raw material for future research which aims to explore the issue of violence from a wider perspective. Later in this chapter, I discuss the need for further research in this area in more detail.

Other empirical research in this area can be seen to follow a similar model: Morrison, MacGregor and Thorpe (1993), Docherty (1990) and Gunter and Wober (1988) all consider viewer response to fictional and factual violence on television through analyzing and exploring qualitative and quantitative data – they do not 'work-up' the results to include larger theoretical issues. However, this is not to say that such a combination of analyses should not be undertaken. Martin Barker (1989) and David Buckingham (1996a) have both published books which investigate the media and society using a number of research methods which prove to be extremely successful in theorizing why, for example, comics and ideology are interlinked, or why the 'video nastie' debate has little to do with how children respond to television. There is room for different types of analysis in this current field of research, and indeed, if the issue of violence is to be explored as it should be, micro and macro levels of analysis are essential to broadening debate in this area.

Another point to be highlighted here, is that this study does not attempt to engage in full dialogue with the literature available on the issue of violence. Chapter 1 briefly touches the tip of the iceberg, but to present an overview of this area would be another book in itself. Buckingham and Allerton (1996b) undertook just such a task, and *A Review of Research on Children's 'Negative' Emotional Responses to Television* is an example of the range and depth such a project must offer. However, at this stage in the book, it seems appropriate to refer to several other studies in this field in order to situate my own findings in relation to the broader framework of research into viewing violence.

There are any number of laboratory and field experiments which this study shares no similarities with (see, for example, Bandura, Ross & Ross [1963],

Feshbach & Singer [1971]). David Gauntlett (1995) has undertaken an exhaustive overview of these experiments, so it is not the place for me to criticize them here. Suffice to say, wiring people up and controlling what they watch is not the aim of this research. Nor does this study have anything to do with 'the desensitization hypothesis' (Van Evra [1990]), or cultivation effects (Gerbner, [1988], Signorielli [1990]). George Gerbner's hypothesis that heavy television viewing leads to a distorted view of society may be considered a direct challenge to my hypothesis that active consumers of violent movies differentiate between real life and watching violent movies. The participants in this study could be classed as 'heavy viewers', but, contrary to Gerbner's claims, they do not develop an unusually high paranoia and fear of crime (see Gerbner, Gross, Morgan and Signorielli [1980, 1986], Signorielli [1990]). The results of this study are more in line with that of Gunter (1985, 1987) and Gunter and Wober (1988) which indicate that viewing violence does not distort perceptions of society, but, rather, reinforces personal experience and opinions regarding violence in society.

A large-scale study by Schlesinger, Dobash, Dobash and Weaver (1992) in women's responses to television violence could be seen as close to my own aims in this book to expand the perception of moviegoers to incorporate male and female consumers of violent movies. Whilst *Women Viewing Violence* offers many interesting results with regard to the way women with (and without) experience of violence respond to depictions of violence on screen, it does not address the question of whether there are women who enjoy watching fictional violent movies. The book, whilst using a representative sample, and purporting to be a wide-reaching and pathbreaking study, examines television violence from the point of view of whether women perceive it as 'beneficial' to be screened on terrestrial television. Hence the key programmes participants discuss in *Women Viewing Violence* are *Crimewatch UK, EastEnders, Closing Ranks* and *The Accused,* all serious, sincere and informative programmes. Whilst analysis of participants' response to these programmes is significant, such a wide-reaching study should have incorporated an example of a programme which contained representations of violence that are, in essence, entertaining. To not include such a programme implies that violence cannot be entertaining. How much more interesting it would be to see if the women in the study differentiated between *The Accused* (Jonathan Kaplan, 1988) and *The Terminator* (James Cameron, 1984), two films which portray violence towards women, but in dramatically different ways.

It is the tradition of research into emotional responses to television that this study is closest to, both in its aims and outcomes. What methods people use when understanding and interpreting television violence has become a significant question in the violence debate, and is one, I suggest, researchers should consider central to an examination of this issue. Qualitative research presents a way for researchers to listen to people who actually watch television. Thus, Morrison, MacGregor and Thorpe (1993, p.86), in *Violence and Factual Television,* talk to people who watch the news and documentary programmes, and discover a number of 'principles governing the response to the broadcasting of factual violence.' Each of these 'principles' represents a method of understanding factual violence which is complex and dynamic. Similarly, David Buckingham (1996a, p.307), in *Moving Images: Understanding Children's Emotional Responses to Television,* finds that on talking to kids who watch horror and melodrama, the children 'develop a variety of "coping strategies" that enable them to avoid or deal with (their) responses.' Such 'coping strategies' include 'partial or total avoidance' and 'actively reinterpreting the text', strategies very similar to those outlined in this book.

Consequently, the results of this study may be un-'theorized' but they represent a significant addition to current research in emotional responses to viewing violence. Perhaps it is best to outline what the results of this study are, before suggesting that these findings can aid our understanding of violence and initiate further research in this area.

Results

The results of this study are difficult to summarize and almost impossible to generalize. As David Buckingham (1996a, p.303) states in *Moving Images: Understanding Children's Emotional Responses to Television*:

> (Qualitative research) is concerned to build theory, and to offer detailed accounts of individual cases rather than to generate causal predictions. It does not easily yield 'findings', or clear statements of proven fact. On the contrary, the temptation is to conclude with the banal observation that everything is terribly complex and contradictory.

The temptation to offer banal statements is very real, and resisting this temptation opens up a whole new area of uncertainty and concern. However, there is little point in undertaking a study such as this if the results have no benefit outside the narrow remit of academic research.

Why people watch violent movies is of enormous importance to the way society views this aspect of the entertainment industry, and the way politicians and the media police viewing material. Understanding the process of viewing violence is one way of opening up current debate concerning the 'effects' of violence to include objective and broad minded responses to this phenomenon of our times. Indeed, perhaps as Martin Barker (1984, 1989) has suggested, we need to change the terms of reference so that instead of using the phrase 'violent movies', one that is heavy with negative implications, a variety of phrases can be adopted which incorporate the multiplicity of responses to the viewing experience. Consequently, I will attempt to bite the bullet and summarize this research with policy recommendations directly in mind. The findings of this study are as follows:

I Violent movies test viewers, and consumers are aware of this

Media hype and peer pressure ensure consumers of violent movies are very much aware that violent movies test viewers. Testing signifies the way in which 'new brutalism' movies challenge audiences with unflinching and realistic portrayals of violence: violence with consequences. It also signifies the way in which 'new brutalism' movies contain intelligent dialogue and direction. It is precisely these factors which draw moviegoers to see these films and make up their own minds about movies which are perceived as dangerous and unhealthy by moral watchdogs in the media and government.

2 Viewing violence is a social activity

Awareness of media hype and peer pressure surrounding these movies ensures that the activity of viewing violence is social. Most viewers I spoke to watched these films either at the cinema or at home, and did not do so alone. Part of the enjoyment of viewing violence is to monitor audience reaction, as the films themselves provoke reaction. Individual response is part of a much wider awareness of the variety of responses available to consumers of violent movies.

3 Anticipation is a key factor in determining response to violence
It is through anticipation that consumers of violent movies are able to choose which method of response they wish to use in order to interpret a violent film or scene. As there are a variety of complex and sophisticated responses to violence, the choice is large, and those viewers I spoke to deliberately anticipated scenes of violence in order to be prepared for individual reactions to violence. This cognitive response of anticipation and preparation is essential to the enjoyment of viewing violent movies.

4 Consumer choice influences character relationships
Identification, in the film theory sense, does not take place during the process of viewing violence. Instead, viewers build a series of character relationships. Those viewers I spoke to built these relationships by utilizing individual experience and imaginative hypothesizing. The phrase: 'if I were in the same situation' is central to the way in which viewers engaged with characters in violent movies. If viewers find specific character(s) too disturbing they choose not to engage with them: this is an act of self-preservation, and part of the safety of viewing violence is that consumers can choose to engage or not engage with characters in violent movies.

5 Thresholds re-affirm social taboos and individual experience
Thresholds are part of the way violent movies test the viewer. Movies use thresholds to provoke reactions, and it is part of the process of viewing violence that participants identify thresholds to violence. Some thresholds are social; they re-affirm social taboos (such as female rape) and signify collective fears. Others are personal and re-affirm individual experience, often based on childhood memories or personal experience of violence. Identifying social or personal thresholds does not necessarily lead to self-censorship. Moviegoers can anticipate and prepare for specific types of fictional violence but choose to not self-censor, such is the function of this reactive mechanism.

6 Viewers use a variety of methods to self-censor violence
There is no one method of self-censoring violence, and viewers draw upon individual preferences, perceived notions of consumers of violent movies, and audience reactions to shape their own method of self-censoring. Those viewers I spoke to activated any number of methods of self-censorship at a given time, looking away from the screen, peeking through their fingers, thinking of the ironing, running out of the room and switching off a video. The way in which viewers prepare to self-censor is the same whether they choose to watch a violent representation or not. The psychological 'location' of thresholds determines the points at which self-censorship occurs.

7 Boundary testing is part of the process of viewing violence
Testing boundaries is a key factor in why people choose to watch violent movies. Through thresholds and self-censorship, and the roles anticipation and preparation have to play in that process, viewers test their own boundaries

whilst viewing violence because it is a safe way of interpreting violence in a fictional setting. Boundary testing is not comparable with 'desensitization'. It arises from reactive mechanisms associated with specific viewing experiences, and is part of the pleasures to be gained from shocking entertainment.

8 Real violence is raw and brutal and not entertaining
Active consumers of violent movies do not find real violence in any way entertaining, and they differentiate between real violence and fictional violence. In many ways, it is because they abhor real violence that those viewers I spoke to chose to watch fictional violence. Once again, it is a safe way of understanding response to violence, without having to experience violence in real life.

9 Fictional violence is entertaining
One of the reasons people choose to see violent movies is because they are entertaining. This does not mean consumers of violent movies find all violence entertaining, but the process of watching a film which is composed of acting, soundtrack, direction, dialogue, as well as representations of violence, is meant to be entertaining because violent movies are part of the entertainment industry and made widely available to the consumer: violent movies aren't free, consumers have to pay for their entertainment as they would with other comparable leisure activities. Those viewers I spoke to thought all the target films could be classed as entertaining, but there are different aspects of entertainment, and some movies are thought more entertaining than others depending on individual preferences, and the stylistic presentation of violence.

10 The safety of violent movies
It is precisely because violent movies are fictional that viewers can feel safe to experience a range of complex and sophisticated responses to violence. They would not be able to do this in any comparable way in real life. Hence, they go to the movies. It is the safety of violent movies which means viewers can utilize portfolios of interpretation. Understanding violence and the ranges of response available is central to the reasons why people choose to watch violent movies. Violence is something all viewers I spoke to feared and abhorred, but this did not mean they eschewed all aspects of violence: it is real violence which is to be avoided, not fictional violence. Consequently, violent movies act as a safe way of exploring the issue of violence and provide a forum for complexities of response.

Portfolios of interpretation
The most significant factor to emerge from the qualitative research is that participants possess what I have termed 'portfolios of interpretation' when viewing violence. The expression 'portfolios of interpretation' signifies the way participants understand and interpret violent movies. It is a metaphor which best describes the accumulation of responses that are part of the viewing process.

The reference to 'portfolios' is reminiscent of folders where art works such as sketches and paintings are contained. These portfolios carry an accumulation of experiences. They may show that the artist is naturally inclined towards still life, or abstract art, and there will be many examples of this experience to confirm this. And every portfolio contains one or two surprises few expect to find because this is the nature of artistic expression. People demonstrate patterns, but never to the extent they can be trusted to do so in a scientific manner.

Thus, portfolios signify a body of work, a record of experiences. The metaphor 'portfolios of interpretation' best sums up the process of viewing violence because moviegoers possess experiences which are multiform. They possess dynamic and fluid methods of response. Some of these methods of response are shared by many others. For example, anticipation is a method of reponse many participants utilize in order to prepare for watching or not watching violence. Other methods of response are shared by few. For example, personal thresholds are unique to each individual, and are utilized in order to re-affirm personal experiences within the context of viewing violence.

However, unlike portfolios used by art students to carry their work, the metaphor 'portfolios of interpretation' implies the *means with which to experience viewing violence*: they contain what moviegoers bring to the viewing environment. Thus, the phrase 'portfolios of interpretation' represents methods of response to viewing violence; these methods are brought to the cinema, or the living room, by the moviegoer and utilized during the viewing event. An active consumer of violent movies may bring with him/her a developed threshold for violence towards women, but it is only once he/she reacts to a scene involving just such a threshold that he/she knows they have utilized this method of response. This is why it is so important to discover the range of responses available to the moviegoer. It is only once we realise what these responses actually are that we can begin to understand the nature of viewing violence and the enjoyment to be gained from this activity.

Portfolios of interpretation, therefore, signify methods of response, but these methods of response are waiting to be activated, and it is only once the moviegoer is within the viewing event that we can begin to record what methods are chosen, and how they are put into operation. I suggest that there are a number of contextual and individual factors which participants draw upon in order to utilize portfolios of interpretation and arrive at a reaction to, or diagnosis of violent movies. I have constructed a model of the viewing process so that these various factors can be presented as clearly as possible.

Model of viewing process

The model of the viewing process is based on the theory of portfolios of interpretation. This model reveals the collective components of the process of viewing violence, and indicates a system of interpretation which can be used as a mechanism for understanding reactions to, or diagnoses of violent movies. Each of the contextual and individual factors significant to before and during the viewing event are true variables. This means that each factor listed in the model of the viewing process is true for every individual, but varies from person to person. If a 'value' for any particular person, or group of people, can be specified, it should be possible to predict their reaction to, or diagnosis of violent films.

Perhaps it is best to provide an example to illustrate this theory. The model of the viewing process has four groups of factors, each significant to one another. Before arriving at the cinema, or settling down to watch a video, the moviegoer brings a number of contextual and individual factors to the pre-viewing event. Thus, for example, a female moviegoer may bring with her a notion that fictional violence is not acceptable as an art form. She may have developed this notion from her family and peers, or from reading newspapers and magazines. Either way, she believes watching screen violence is like watching real violence

Model of viewing process

Pre-viewing
Contextual Factors

a. Societal/normative
   notions of
   acceptability of
   violent images
b. Cinema
   going/video
   viewing as learned
   social behaviour

Within Viewing Event
Contextual Factors

a. Safety of Cinema
b. Context of event
   as social activity
c. Testing by film

Pre-viewing
Individual Factors

c. Conceptualization
   of fictional violence
   as entertaining
d. Perceptions of real
   violence
e. Anticipation (Pre-
   viewing)
f. Developed
   thresholds

Within Viewing Event
Individual Factors

d. Anticipation
   (Whilst viewing)
e. Building character
   relationships
f. Thresholds
g. Self-censorship
h. Boundary testing

Outcome

Reaction to,
diagnosis of
violent film

Model of male viewing process

Pre-viewing
Contextual Factors

a. Societal/normative
   notions of
   acceptability of
   violent images
   = *Unacceptable*
b. Cinema
   going/video
   viewing as learned
   social behaviour
   = *Manifest*

Within Viewing Event
Contextual Factors

a. Safety of Cinema
   = *Utilized*
b. Context of event
   as social activity
   = *Low awareness*
c. Testing by film
   = *Acknowledged*

Pre-viewing
Individual Factors

c. Conceptualization
   of fictional violence
   as entertaining
   = *Popular leisure
   activity*
d. Perceptions of real
   violence
   = *Abhorrent/not
   entertaining*
e. Anticipation (Pre-
   viewing)
   = *Palpable*
f. Developed
   thresholds
   = *Not apparent*

Within Viewing Event
Individual Factors

d. Anticipation
   (Whilst viewing)
   = *Utlized (to watch)*
e. Building character
   relationships
   = *Dynamic and
   fluid*
f. Thresholds
   = *Low awareness*
g. Self-censorship
   = *Low levels*
h. Boundary testing
   = *High levels –
   essential to viewing
   process*

Outcome

Reaction to, diagnosis
of violent film:
challenging and
entertaining

Model of female viewing process

Pre-viewing
Contextual Factors

Within Viewing Event
Contextual Factors

a. Societal/normative
   notions of
   acceptability of
   violent images
   = *Unacceptable*
b. Cinema
   going/video viewing
   as learned social
   behaviour
   = *Manifest*

a. Safety of Cinema
   = *Utilized*
b. Context of event
   as social activity
   = *High awareness*
c. Testing by film
   = *Acknowledged*

Pre-viewing
Individual Factors

Within Viewing Event
Individual Factors

c. Conceptualization
   of fictional violence
   as entertaining
   = *Atypical leisure
   activity*
d. Perceptions of real
   violence
   = *Abhorrent/not
   entertaining*
e. Anticipation (Pre-
   viewing)
   = *Palpable*
f. Developed
   thresholds
   = *Apparent*

d. Anticipation
   (Whilst viewing)
   = *Utlized (not watch)*
e. Building character
   relationships
   = *Dynamic and fluid*
f. Thresholds
   = *High awareness*
g. Self-censorship
   = *High levels*
h. Boundary testing
   = *High levels –
   essential to viewing
   process*

Outcome

Reaction to, diagnosis
of violent film:
challenging and
entertaining

and she therefore considers this unacceptable behaviour. Once this moviegoer settles down to watch the film, she is within the viewing event. Let us say she is at the cinema watching *Man Bites Dog*, but she believes it is a movie about dogs, not serial killers. We can predict her reaction based on the number of individual factors she will draw upon in order to respond to this movie. The methods of response available include anticipation and self-censorship. We can already ascertain from her perception of this movie as a film about dogs that her anticipation (pre-viewing) is not in accordance with the actual content of the movie. Thus her anticipation (whilst viewing) is completely overturned when, rather than seeing a scene about a man and his dog, she sees a serial killer and his prey. Her reaction will be one of disgust and abhorrence, and she will utilize the reactive mechanism of self-censorship and walk out of the cinema. In a sense, we can predict her reaction based on the contextual and individual factors relevant to her experience, and we can arrive at a diagnosis of this movie as not entertaining because of her reaction to this film.

Of course, I have chosen an extreme example in order to best illustrate the way in which the model of the viewing process can be used. What I want to point out is that we would not be able to predict this viewer's reaction to this film if we did not already have an understanding of the portfolios of interpretation this moviegoer carries with them. If another moviegoer perceived violent movies as entertaining, and liked films about serial killers, then we may be able to predict their reaction to the film as one of involvement and interest. We have only been able to reach this outcome through examining the contextual and individual factors significant to before and during the viewing event and placing a 'value' next to those factors relevant the viewing experience. It is only when viewers utilize certain methods of response, such as anticipation, or boundary testing, that it is possible to see how complex and dynamic the process of viewing violence actually is.

This system of understanding and interpreting reactions to violent films can be used with policy recommendations directly in mind. However, it should be noted that this model of the viewing process is based on a specific category of viewer, one that is an active consumer of violent movies. It is not within the remit of this book to refine the model to include all types of moviegoers. This is a job for further research in this area. Thus, the model of the viewing process, refined in two separate models to indicate the reactions to violent films by male and female participants, is specific to this study. This study concludes with a series of policy recommendations which are of direct relevance to social, political and cultural parties who are interested in the future of violent films.

Further research
The theory of 'portfolios of interpretation' does not need to remain within the confines of this study. The focus groups generated hypotheses regarding viewing violence, and this led me to construct a theory of the viewing process based on methods of response to the viewing experience. This research represents the 'micro-level' of analysis. However, further research can incorporate wider issues and concerns. There are issues touched on in this study which would benefit from further investigation. For example, the contextual factor of the social activity of viewing violence could be incorporated within a larger framework of theoretical analysis which would attempt to investigate why viewing violence is a social activity, and how this may influence our attitudes

to art forms in our present cultural climate. This type of research would represent the 'macro-level' of analysis.

Consequently, the second stage of this research will focus on the theoretical issues raised in this sociological study. Central to this second stage of research will be the significance of boundary testing as a pleasurable activity. Reactive mechanisms such as self-censorship are developed in order to test boundaries within the confines of the leisure industry. Watching TV, going to the cinema, reading books: these are all leisure activities which in certain circumstances, and with certain types of material, demand reactive mechanisms which lead to boundary testing. This is a social activity and it is in our interests to attempt to understand the popularity of this phenomenon. This is not to say that empirical research does not have a further role to play in understanding the nature of shocking entertainment – more research in this area would only serve to strengthen the results put forward in this study. However, a combination of micro and macro levels of analysis will achieve rich results and signify the breadth of investigation necessary when examining the issue of violence.

Policy recommendations

There are a number of policy recommendations to be made regarding the results of this research and attitudes to screening violent movies:

- The debate about 'violence' needs to acknowledge complexities of response when viewing violent movies.
- It should be openly acknowledged that violent movies are part of the entertainment industry and consumers choose to see them because they are entertaining.
- Centralised censorship should be made accountable and the rationale for policy decisions made available to the public.
- The role self-censorship has to play in the viewing process should be taken into account by the government and self-appointed 'moral watchdogs' and, in particular, regulators such as the British Board of Film Classification, and the Independent Television Commission.

Consumers of violent movies possess portfolios of interpretation and the 'effects' debate needs to explore what this signifies in relation to response to violence, as there is no one response to viewing violence, but varieties of response which are activated by the consumer, not by movies themselves.

Appendix 1
Guiding Questions for Focus Groups

I Introduction
There are name cards around the table and I'd like to ask you to introduce yourself and tell us the most recent film you saw on the list in front of you.

II Opening Question

1 How do you choose to see these movies?

   A) How do they compare to other films like the *Die Hard* series, or *Terminator 2*?

III Transition Question

2 Going to the cinema is a social activity; do you notice how other people respond to violent scenes in a film?

3 What physical emotions do you feel when you see a violent scene in a film?

   A) Can you anticipate the violence in a film?

IV Key Questions

Characterization

CUE: *Henry, Portrait of a Serial Killer* – eye-stabbing scene

4 Do you identify with any one character in this scene?

5 Is it necessary to know something about the characters before you are able to identify with one of them?

Thresholds and Self-censorship

6 What do you think to the visual effects of violence in these films?

CUE: *Reservoir Dogs* – ear-amputation scene

7 What is your personal response to this scene?

A) Would you, or anyone you know not watch this scene?

B) What would be the reason?

8 Would you not watch a scene in a film you found disturbing?

A) What would be the reason?

Entertainment

9 How does these movies compare to watching real violence on the news, or in real life?

10 Are these films entertaining?

CUE: List of target films.

V Summary and Conclusion

12 Summary of key questions.

13 Invite comments.

Appendix 2
List of Target Films Used in Focus Groups

List of Target Films

Reservoir Dogs

Pulp Fiction

True Romance

Natural Born Killers

Man Bites Dog

Henry, Portrait of a Serial Killer

Bad Lieutenant

Killing Zoe

Appendix 3
Registration Form – Focus Groups

NAME ———————————————————————————

AGE ————————————————————————————

MALE/FEMALE —————————————————————————

ETHNIC ORIGIN ————————————————————————

EDUCATIONAL QUALIFICATIONS —————————————————

PLEASE TICK WHICH FILMS YOU HAVE SEEN

Reservoir Dogs ☐

Pulp Fiction ☐

True Romance ☐

Natural Born Killers ☐

Man Bites Dog ☐

Henry, Portrait of a Serial Killer ☐

Bad Lieutenant ☐

Killing Zoe ☐

PLEASE INDICATE WHICH FILMS YOU HAVE SEEN AT THE
CINEMA, ON VIDEO, OR BOTH. USE C FOR CINEMA OR V FOR
VIDEO, AND WRITE THE CORRESPONDING LETTER NEXT TO
EACH FILM

WHICH CINEMAS DO YOU REGULARLY GO TO?————————

—————————————————————————————

WHAT PAPERS/MAGAZINES DO YOU REGULARLY READ? ————

—————————————————————————————

Bibliography

Articles and Books

Andrew, G, 1994. 'Killing Joke' *Time Out*, September 21-28, p.24-26.

Bandura, A, Ross, D, and Ross, S, A, 1963. 'Imitation of Film-Mediated Aggressive Models' in *Journal of Personality and Social Psychology*. Vol.66, pp.3-11.

Barker, M, ed., 1984. *The Video Nasties: Freedom and Censorship in the Media*. London: Pluto Press.

Barker, M, 1989. *Comics: Ideology, Power and the Critics*. Manchester: Manchester University Press.

Barlow, G, and Hill, A, eds., 1985. *Video Violence and Children*. London: Hodder and Stoughton.

Barratt, J, 1996. *VideoWATCH*. London: British Film Institute and Middlesex University.

Bateman, L, 1993. 'Dogs Impounded as BBFC shows teeth' in *Screen International*, Friday April 2, p.6.

Bell, D, Caplan, P, and Karim, W. J., eds., 1993. *Gendered Fields: Women, Men and Ethnography*. London: Routledge.

Belson, W, 1978. *Television Violence and the Adolescent Boy*. Farnborough: Saxon House.

Bordwell, D, 1985. *Narration in the Fiction Film*. London: Routledge.

Bordwell, D, 1989. *Making Meaning: Inference and Rhetoric in the Interpretation of Cinema*. America: Harvard University Press.

Boston, R, 1994. 'Sense and Censorship' in the *Guardian*. 7 April 1994, section 2, p.5.

Bryant, J, and Zillmann, D, eds., 1991. *Responding to the Screen: Reception and Reaction Processes*. Hillsdale, New Jersy: Lawrence Erlbaum.

Buckingham, D, 1993a. *Children Talking Television: An Overview of the Literature*. London: BFI Mimeograph.

Buckingham, D, 1993b. *Reading Audiences: Young People and the Media*. Manchester: Manchester University Press.

Buckingham, D, 1996a. *Moving Images: Understanding Children's Emotional Responses to Television.* Manchester: Manchester University Press.

Buckingham, D & Allerton, M, 1996b. *A Review of Research on Children's 'Negative' Emotional Responses to Television. Research Working Paper 12.* London: Broadcasting Standards Council.

Burt, C, 1925. *The Young Delinquent.* London: The University of London Press.

Cantor, J, Ziemke, C, and Sparks, C, 1984. 'Effects of Forwarning on Emotional Responses to a Horror Film' in *Journal Of Broadcasting.* 28, 1, pp.21-31.

Carroll, N, 1990. *The Philosophy of Horror, or Paradoxes of the Heart.* London: Routledge.

Church, M, 1993. 'Colours of the Charnel House' in the *Observer*, Review section. 8th January, 1993, p.33.

Clover, C, 1992. *Men, Women and Chain Saws.* 2nd edition (1993), London: British Film Institute.

Cohen, S, 1972. *Folk Devils and Moral Panics: the Creation of the Mods and Rockers.* London: MacGibbon and Kee.

Cohen, S, and Young, J, eds, 1973. *The Manufacture of News: Deviance, Social Problems and the Mass Media.* London: Constable.

Cox, P, 1993. 'Gore Blimey Keitel's Back' in the *Sun.* 19 February 1993, p.19.

Creed, B, 1993. *The Monstrous Feminine: Film, Feminism, Psychoanalysis.* London: Routledge.

Culf, A, 1996. 'V-Chip Would Be No "Magic Bullet" Warns US Expert', the *Guardian*, March 27, 1996, p.7.

Cumberbatch, G and Howitt, D, 1989. *A Measure of Uncertainty: the Effects of the Mass Media.* London: John Libbey & Company Ltd.

Dargis, M, 1994. 'Pulp Instincts' in *Sight and Sound*, Vol.4, Issue 5, May 1994, p.6.

Denzin, N, K, 1970. *The Research Act.* Chicago: Aldline.

Docherty, D, Morrison, D, and Tracey, M, 1987. *The Last Picture Show: Britain's Changing Film Audience.* London: British Film Institute.

Docherty, D, 1990. *Violence in Television Fiction:* Broadcasting Standards Council Annual Review. London: John Libbey and Company Ltd.

Easton-Ellis, B, 1991. *American Psycho.* London: Picador.

Edwards, M, 1994. 'Censorship' in The Face. No. 69, June 1994, pp.62-66.

Electric Pictures, 1992. *Henry, Portrait of a Serial Killer.* London: Electric Pictures (Distributed by FoxVideo, subsidiary).

Elton, B, 1996. *Popcorn.* London: Simon & Schuster.

Ferman, 1994, 'At the Sharp End' in *Empire*, no 59, May, p.90.

Feshbach, S, and Singer, R, D, 1971. *Television and Aggression: An Experimental Field Study.* San Francisco: Jossey-Bass.

Fielding, N, G, and Fielding, J, L, 1986. *Linking Data.* Beverly Hills: Sage.

Finch, J, 1993. 'It's Great to Have Someone to Talk to: The Ethics and Politics of Interviewing Women' in M. Hammersley, ed., *Social Research: Philosophy, Politics and Practice*. pp.166-80. London: Sage.

Floyd, N, 1992. 'Dog Days' in *Time Out*, 30th December 1992 - 6th January 1993, p.16.

Freeland, C and Wartenburg, N, eds, 1995. *Philosophy and Film*. London: Routledge.

Freeland, C, 1995. 'Realist Horror' in Freeland, C & Wartenburg, N, eds, 1995. *Philosophy and Film*. London: Routledge.

French, S, 1993. 'Cut and Run is Wrong' in the *Observer*, 18 July 1993, p.53.

Gauntlett, D, 1995. *Moving Experiences: Understanding Television's Influences and Effects*. London: John Libbey.

Gauntlett, D, 1997. *Video Critical: Children, the Environment and Media Power*. London: John Libbey Media.

Gerbner, G, Gross, L, Morgan, M, Signorielli, N, 1980. 'The 'Mainstreaming' of America: Violence Profile No.11' in *Journal of Communication*. Vol. 30, No.3, pp.10-29.

Gerbner, G, Gross, L, Morgan, M, Signorielli, N, 1986. 'Living With Television: The Dynamics of the Cultivation Process' in Bryant, J, and Zillman, D, eds. *Perspectives on Media Effects*. Hillsdale, New Jersey: Lawrence Erlbaum Associates.

Gerbner, G, 1988. *Violence and Terror in the Mass Media*. Unesco Reports and Papers on Mass Communication No.102, Paris: Unesco.

Gerbner, G, 1994. 'The Politics of Media Violence: Some Reflections', in LinnÈ, Olga, & Hamelink, Cees, J, eds. *Mass Communication Research: On Problems and Policies: The Art of Asking the Right Questions*. New Jersey: Ablex Publishing.

Giddens, A, 1976. *New Rules of Sociological Method: A Positive Critique of Interpretative Sociologies*. London: Hutchinson.

Giddens, A, 1991. *Modernity and Self-Identity: Self and Society in the Late Modern Age*. Cambridge: Polity Press.

Gillespie, M, 1995. *Television, Ethnicity, and Cultural Change*. London: Routledge.

Goldman, A, E, and McDonald, S, S, 1987. *The Group Depth Interview: Principles and Practices*. Englewood Cliffs, New Jersy: Prentice-Hall.

Goodwin, P, 1994. 'You've Been Framed' in *Broadcast*. 22 April, 1994, p.15.

Gray, A, 1992. *Video Playtime: the Gendering of a Leisure Technology*. London: Routledge.

Greenbaum, T, L, 1987. *The Practical Handbook and Guide to Focus Group Research*. Lexington, MA: Lexington Books.

Grixti, J, 1989. *The Terrors of Uncertainty*. London: Routledge.

Gunter, B, 1985. *Dimensions of Television Violence*. Aldershot: Gower.

Gunter, B, 1987. *Television and the Fear of Crime*. London: John Libbey and Company Ltd.

Gunter, B, and Wober, M, 1988. *Violence on Television: What the Viewers*

Think. London: John Libbey and Company Ltd.

Guttridge, P, 1993. 'Are These Films Too Violent' in the *Daily Telegraph*. 22 January 1993, p.18.

Hagell, A, and Newburn, T, 1994. *Young Offenders and the Media: Viewing Habits and Preferences*. London: Policy Studies Institute.

Hoffman, D, 1996. 'Dustin Hoffman Blames Hollywood Over Dunblane' *The Independent*, Saturday 11th May, 1996, p.6.

Hughes, J, A, 1990. *The Philosophy of Social Research: Second Edition*. London: Longman.

Katz, E, 1992. *The Macmillan International Film Encyclopedia*. London: Macmillan.

Kidd-Hewitt, D, and Osborne, R, 1995. *Crime and the Media: the Postmodern Perspective*. London: Pluto Press

Kirk, J, and Miller, M, L, 1986. *Reliability and Validity of Qualitative Research*. Sage University Paper, Qualitative Research Methods Series, Vol.1. Beverly Hills, CA: Sage.

Krueger, R, A, 1988. *Focus Groups: a Practical Guide for Applied Research*. Newbury Park, CA: Sage.

Lazarus, R, S, 1975. 'The Self-regulation of Emotion' in *Emotions: Their Parameters and Measurement*. New York: Raven Press.

Lazarus, R, S, and Folkman, S, 1984. *Stress, Appraisal and Coping*. New York: Springer.

Lisle, de, L, 1995. 'An Unhealthy Intimacy With Violence' in the *Independent on Sunday*, 11 June 1995, p.27.

Livingston, S, M, 1990. *Making Sense of Television: the Psychology of Audience Interpretation*. Oxford: Pergamon Press.

Malcolm, D, 1993a. *Man Bites Dog*. London: Tartan Video.

Malcolm, D, 1993b. 'Dogs of Gore' in the *Guardian*, 7 January, 1993, p.6.

Mannheim, H, 1970. *Comparative Criminology II*. London: Routledge and Kegan Paul.

Martin, J, 1993. *The Seduction of the Gullible*. Nottingham: Procrustes Press.

May, T, 1993. *Social Research: Issues, Methods and Process*. Buckingham: Open University Press.

Mayne, J, 1993. *Cinema and Spectatorship*. London: Routledge.

McKee, L, and O'Brien, M, 1983. 'Interviewing Men: "Taking Gender Seriously"' in E. Gamarnikow, D.H.J.

Medved, M, 1992. *Hollywood vs America: Popular Culture and the War on Traditional Values*. New York: HarperCollins.

Middleton, R, 1995. 'Zombie Film Eater: Interview with Lucio Fulci' in *Samhain*. Issue 50, May/June 1995, pp.7-10.

Millwood-Hargrave, A, 1993. *Violence in Factual Television: Broadcasting Standards Council Annual Review*. London: John Libbey and Company Ltd.

Moores, S, 1993. *Interpreting Audiences: The Ethnography of Media Consumption*. London: Sage.

Morgan, D.L, 1988. *Focus Groups as Qualitative Research.* London: Sage Publications.

Morgan, J, Purvis, D, and Taylorson, eds., *The Public and the Private.* London: Heinemann.

Morrison, D, MacGregor, B, and Thorpe, A, 1993. 'Detailed Findings of the Editing Groups' in *Violence in Factual Television.* London: John Libbey and Company Ltd.

Morrison, D, 1993. 'The Idea of Violence' in Hargrave, A, M, ed., *Violence in Factual Television.* London: John Libbey and Company Ltd.

Morrison, R, 1996. 'Who Supports Violent Films Now?' *The Times,* Saturday, March 16, p.17.

Newson, E, 1994. 'Video Violence and the Protection of Children', mimeo, Child Development Research Unit, University of Nottingham.

Nilsson, T, 1993, 'Quentin Tarantino Interview' in *Samhain.* Issues 36 & 37, Jan/Feb, Mar/Apr 1993, pp.12-15, pp.12-13.

Oliver, M, B, 1993. 'Adolescents' Enjoyment of Graphic Horror: Effects of Viewers' Attitudes and Portrayals of Victims' in *Communication Research.* 20, 1, pp.30-50.

Padfield, M, and Procter, I, 1996. 'The Effect of Interviewers' Gender on the Interview Process: A Comparative Enquiry' in *Sociology.* Vol.30, no.2, May 1996, pp.355-366.

Palmer, P, 1986. *The Lively Audience: A Study of Children Around the TV Set.* Sydney: Allen & Unwin.

Pearson, G, 1983. *Hooligan: A History of Respectable Fears.* London: Macmillan.

Rich, B, R, 1992. 'Art House Killers' *Sight and Sound,* Vol.2, No.8, December, pp.5-6.

Romney, J, 1993. 'One Way Ticket to Hell' in *New Statesman and Society.* 19 February 1993, pp.34-35.

Sargeant, J, 1995. *Deathtripping: the Cinema of Transgression.* London: Creation Books.

Schlesinger, P, Dobash, R, E, Dobash, R, P, and Weaver, C, K, 1992. *Women Viewing Violence.* London: British Film Institute.

Seiter, E, Borchers, H, Kreutzner, G, Warth, E, eds., 1989. *Remote Control: Television, Audiences and Cultural Power.* London and New York: Routledge.

Shelley, J, 1993a. 'The Boys Are Back in Town' in the *Guardian.* 7 January 1993, p.7.

Shelley, J, 1993b. 'Down These Mean Streets Many Men Have Gone' in *The Times,* Saturday Review. 20 February, 1993, p.12.

Sigal, C, 1993. 'Killing Jokes' The *Guardian Weekend* Magazine, September 11, p.24-28.

Signorielli, N, 1990. 'Television's Mean and Dangerous World: A Continuation of the Cultural Indicators Perspective' in Signorielli, N, and Morgan, M, eds., 1990. *Cultivation Analysis: New Directions in Media Effects Research.* Newbury Park, California: Sage.

Singer, D, and Singer, J, L, 1983. 'Learning How to be Intelligent Consumers of Television' in Howe, M, J, A, ed., *Learning From Television: Psychological and Educational Research.* London: Academic Press.

Smith, M, 1995. *Engaging Characters: Fiction, Emotion, and the Cinema.* Oxford: Oxford University Press.

Sparks, G, G, 1986. 'Developing a Scale to Assess Cognitive Responses to Frightening Films' in *Journal of Broadcasting and Electronic Media.* 30, 1, pp.65-73.

Sparks, G, G, 1989. 'Understanding Emotional Reactions to a Suspenseful Movie: the Interaction Between Forewarning and Preferred Coping Style' in *Communication Monographs.* 56, 4, pp. 325-340.

Sparks, G, G, 1991. 'The Relationship Between Distress and Delight in Males' and Females' Reactions to Frightening Films' in *Human Communication Research.* 17, 4, pp.625-637.

Tamborini, R, and Stiff, J, 1987. 'Predictors of Horror Film Attendance and Appeal: an Analysis of the Audience for Frightening Films' in *Communication Research.* 14, 4, pp. 415-436.

Tamborini, R, Stiff, J, and Heidel, C, 1990. 'Reacting to Graphic Horror: a Model of Empathy and Emotional Behaviour' in *Communication Research.* 17, 5, pp.616-640.

Tarantino, Q, 1994a. *Reservoir Dogs.* London: Faber and Faber.

Tarantino, Q, 1994b. *Pulp Fiction.* London: Faber and Faber.

Tullock, J, and Tulloch, M, 1992. 'Discourses About Violence: Critical Theory and the "TV Violence" Debate' in Text. Vol 12, no.2, pp.183-231.

Usher, S, 1992. 'Deadly Dogs Unleash a Whirlwind of Violence' in the *Daily Mail.* 22 December 1992, p.26.

Van Evra, J, 1990. *Television and Child Development.* Hillsdale, New Jersy: Lawrence Erlbaum Associates.

Walker, A, 1992. 'Shooting the Dogs of Gore' in the *Evening Standard,* 5 November 1992, pp.43-44.

Wark, P, and Ball, S, 1996. 'Death of Innocence' in *The Sunday Times,* 23 June 1996, p.12.

Welsh, I, 1995. *Marabou Stork Nightmares.* London: Vintage.

Wiegman, O, Kuttschreuter, M, and Baarda, B, 1992. 'A Longitudinal Study of the Effects of Television Viewing on Aggressive and Pro-social Behaviours' in *British Journal of Social Psychology.* Vol.31, pp.147-164.

Wintour, P, and Bunting, M, 1996. 'Natural Born Killers Video Held Back' The *Guardian,* March 14 1996, p.5.

Wober, M, and Gunter, B, 1987. *Television and Social Control.* Avebury: Gower.

Wood, R, 1978. 'Gods and Monsters' in *Film Comment.* Vol. 14, no.5, pp.19-25.

Wood, R, 1980. 'Neglected Nightmares' in *Film Comment.* Vol. 16, no.2, pp.25-28.

Zillman, D, Weaver, J, B, Mundorf, N, and Aust, C, F, 1986. 'Effects of an

Opposite-gender Companion's Affect to Horror on Distress, Delight and Attraction' in *Journal of Personality and Social Psychology.* 51, 3, pp. 586-594.

Filmography

Accused, The, 1988, Jonathan Kaplan

Bad Lieutenant, 1992, Abel Ferrara

Braveheart, 1995, Mel Gibson

Clockwork Orange, A, 1971, Stanley Kubrick

Die Hard, 1988, John McTiernan

Die Hard 2, 1990, John McTiernan

Die Hard with a Vengeance, 1995, John McTiernan

Exorcist, The, 1973, William Friedkin

Henry, Portrait of a Serial Killer, John McNaughton, 1990 (Prod. 1986)

Killing Zoe, 1994, Roger Avary

Last House on the Left, 1972, Wes Craven

Man Bites Dog, 1992, Belvaux, Bonzel, Poelvoorde

Misery, 1990, Rob Reiner

Nightmare on Elm Street, A, 1984, Wes Craven

Natural Born Killers, 1994, Oliver Stone

Outbreak, 1995, Wolfgang Petersen

Pretty Woman, 1990, Gary Marshall

Pulp Fiction, 1994, Quentin Tarantino

Reservoir Dogs, 1992, Quentin Tarantino

Schindler's List, 1993, Steven Spielberg

Shining, The, 1980, Stanley Kubrick

Straw Dogs, 1971, Sam Peckinpah

Terminator, The, 1984, James Cameron

Terminator 2: Judgment Day, 1991, James Cameron

Texas Chain Saw Massacre, The, 1974, Tobe Hooper

Thelma and Louise, 1991, Ridley Scott

True Romance, 1993, Tony Scott

Twin Peaks: Fire Walk with Me, 1992, David Lynch

Index

Accused, The, 53, 54, 103
Alabama (Patricia Arquette), 36, 52, 53
Alton, D., 2, 9
American Psycho, 65
Andrew, G., 10, 88
anticipation, 34–36, 65, 66, 96–7
audience awareness, 27, 28–32
audio/visual effects, 95–98
Avary, R, 10, 127

Bad Lieutenant, 82, 83
Baltz, K., 86, 87, 92–95
Bandura, A, et al, 102
Barker, M., 8, 12, 102, 104
Barlow, G, and Hill, A, 1
Barratt, J., 7, 8
Bateman, L, 88
Becky (Tracy Arnold), 45–8
Bell, D, et al, 16
Belson, W, 12
Belvaux, Bonzel, Poelvoorde, 10, 127
boundary testing, 65–73, 96–100
Bordwell, D, 4
Braveheart, 28, 30
Boston, R, 121
Bryant, J, and Zillmann, D, 121, 123
Buckingham, D., and Zillmann, 102
Buckingham, D., 4, 8, 102, 103–104
building character relationships, 39–50
Burt, C., 3
Butch (Bruce Willis), 35

Caan J, 72
Cameron, J, 103
Cantor, J, et al, 2
Carroll, N, 4, 7

Church, M, 87
Cinema Advertising Association, 13, 14
cinematic environment, 27, 62–64
Clockwork Orange, A, 59
Clover, C, 4, 7
Cohen, S, 3
Cohen and Young, 3
consumer choice, 19–26
Cox, P, 10
Creed, B, 7
Craven, W., 87
critical response, 98–100
Culf, A, 9
Cumberbatch, G and Howitt, D, 1

Dargis, M, 10
Denzin, N, K, 9
desensitization, 11, 12, 68, 69, 77, 99
Die Hard series, 22, 23
Docherty, D, 13, 102
Docherty, D, et al, 1

ear-amputation scene, 16, 66, 72
Edwards, M, 122
Electric Pictures, 10
Elton, B., 3
emotional involvement, 78–81
emotional response, 32. 33. 98–100
entertainment, 75–85
Exorcist, The, 57, 127
eye-stabbing scene (Henry, Portrait of ...), 16,
   39–49, 86–100

Ferman, J., 11, 88
Ferrara, 10, 127
Feshbach, S, and Singer, R, D, 103

Fielding, N, G, and Fielding, J, L, 9
Finch, J, 16
Floyd, N, 87
Friedkin, W, 127
Freeland, C. A., 3, 7
Freeland, C and Wartenburg, N, 4
French, S, 88
Fulci, L, 88, 124

Gauntlett, D., 2, 7–8, 103
gender difference, 16, 23, 30–32, 67–71
Gerbner, G., 3, 103
Gerbner, G, et al, 105
Gibson, M, 28, 127
Giddens, A, 9
Gillespie, M, 8
Goldman, A, E, and McDonald, S, S, 9
Goodwin, P., 9
Gray, A., 8
Greenbaum, T, L, 9
Grixti, J, 7
Gunter, B, 103
Gunter, B, and Wober, M, 13, 102, 103
Guttridge, P, 11

Hagell, A, and Newburn, T, 12
Hargrave, A, M., 4
Henry (Michael Rooker), 45, 46
Henry, Portrait of a Serial Killer, 39–49, 83
Hoffman, D., 1
Hollywood action movies, 24, 25
holocaust, the, 80
home environment, 28, 61–64
Hooper, T, 29, 127
Hughes, J, A, 9

identification, 41
imaginative hypothesizing, 43–49, 89–98

Kaplan, J, 53, 103
Katz, E., 10
Keitel, H., 10, 86
Kermode, M, 91
Kidd-Hewitt, D, and Osborne, R, 3
Killing Zoe, 10, 14, 18, 20, 25, 64–65, 117–118, 127
Kirk, J, and Miller, M, L, 7
Krueger, R, A, 7, 9
Kubrick, S, 59

Last House on the Left, 87
Lazarus, R, S, 2

Lazarus, R, S, and Folkman, S, 2
Lisle, de, T., 88
Livingston, S, M, 1

Madsen, M., 86–91, 95
Malcolm, D., 10, 88
male rape , 35
Man Bites Dog, 62, 83–85
Mannheim, H., 4
Marabou Stork Nightmares, 64
Marcellus (Vick Rhames), 35, 54
Marshall, G, 54
Martin, J, 3, 124
Marvin (Kirk Baltz), 86–100
Marvin scene (Pulp Fiction), 29
May, T, 9
Mayne, J, 1
McKee, L, and O'Brien, M, 16
McNaughton, J, 39
McTiernan, J, 127
media hype, 21
mediated images of violence, 75–85
Medved, M., 3
mental barriers, 59, 60
Middleton, R, 87
Misery, 72
Model of the Viewing Process, 5, 107–112
monitoring response, 22
monitoring audience reaction, 27
Moores, S., 1, 7
moral panics, 3
Morgan, D, L., 7, 9
Morgan, J, et al, 104, 123–25
Morrison, D, et al, 104, 105
Morrison, R, 4
Mr Blonde (Michael Madsen), 86–100
Mr Orange (Tim Roth), 86, 87, 92
Mr White (Harvey Keitel), 86
Mr Pink (Steve Buscemi), 86

Natural Born Killers, 1, 82
new brutalism, 9–11, 24, 25
news footage, 77, 78
Newson, E., 1, 2
Nice Guy Eddie (Chris Penn), 86
Nicholson, D. (MP), 3
Nightmare on Elm Street, A., 69, 87
Nilsson, T, 87
Norman, N, 89

Oliver, M, B, 4
Otis (Tom Towles), 40, 42, 45

Outbreak, 60

Padfield, M, and Procter, I, 16
Palmer, P, 1, 8
Pearson, G, 3
peer pressure, 21
Peckinpah, S, 54
personal experience, 43, 56, 57, 94
personal thresholds, 56–58
Petersen, W, 127
physical barriers, 59, 60
physical emotions, 32, 33
Polanski, R., 65
portfolios of interpretation, 4, 106, 107
Pretty Woman, 54
Pulp Fiction, 23, 55

qualitative research, 7–17, 102–112

real violence, 78–81, 156–58
Reiner, R, 127
repeated viewing, 98–100
Reservoir Dogs, 23, 60, 61, 86–100
Rich, B, R., 11
Romney, J., 10

Sargeant, J, 7
Schindler's List, 80
Schlesinger, P. et al, 4, 8, 103
Scott, R, 89
Scott, T, 10, 127
Seiter, E, et al, 1
self-censorship, 51–73, 96
Shining, The, 71
Shelley, J., 11
Sigal, C, 10
Signorielli, N, 103
Singer, D, and Singer, J, L, 2, 104, 122, 126

Smith, M, 4
social taboos, 55
social thresholds, 52–56
social threshold of rape, 52–55
Sparks, G, G, 2, 4
Spielberg, S, 80
Stealers Wheel, 89, 95
Stone, O, 1
Straw Dogs, 1, 54

Tamborini, R, and Stiff, J, 2
Tarantino, Q., 10, 87, 88
Tate, S., 65
Terminator, 105
Terminator 2, 24
Thelma and Louise, 89
True Romance, 52, 61, 70
Tullock, J, and Tulloch, M, 1
Twin Peaks, 59

Usher, S., 10, 87, 88

Van Evra, J, 103
V-chip, 2
video nasties, 102
'violence', 11, 12
violence and guns, 36
violence towards children and animals, 55

Walker, A., 10, 87
Wark, P, and Ball, S, 2
Welsh, I., 64
Wiegman, O, et al, 1
Winner, M., 4
Wintour, P, and Bunting, M, 9
Wood, R, 7

Zillman, D, et al, 4